REFORMING RELIGIOUS EDUCATION

Bedord Way Series
Published by Kogan Page in association with the Institute of Education,
University of London

Some forthcoming titles:

THE BEDFORD WAY SERIES

REFORMING RELIGIOUS EDUCATION

The Religious Clauses of the 1988 Education Reform Act

EDWIN COX AND JOSEPHINE M CAIRNS

KOGAN PAGE

Published in association with
The Institute of Education, University of London

First published in 1989 by Kogan Page Ltd.,
120 Pentonville Road, London N1 9JN

Typeset from Authors' disk by Saxon Printing Ltd., Derby.
Printed and bound in Great Britain by Biddles Ltd., Guildford

British Library Cataloguing in Publication Data
Cox, Edwin
  Reforming religious education: the religious
  clauses of the 1988 Education Reform Act.
  1. England. Schools. Religious education. Law. Law
  of religious education in schools. Great Britain.
  Education Act 1988
  344.204'796

  ISBN 1-85091-898-8

Contents

Notes on Contributors

Josephine M. Cairns is a Lecturer at the University of London Institute of Education, in charge of the religious education courses. She also acts as Adviser to students at the Institute.

Edwin Cox is Emeritus Reader in Education at the University of London and Associate Fellow of the University of Warwick.

Riadh El-Droubie is Director of Minaret House and a member of the Shap Working Party and of Interfaith Dialogue. He has written a number of books to help the teaching of Islam in schools.

Alastair Falk is Head of the Independent Jewish Day School, a voluntary aided Jewish primary school in the London Borough of Barnet.

V. P. Kanitkar, after many years as a teacher, has devoted his time in recent years to writing books about Hinduism for use in schools. For these books he has used the name Hemant Kanitkar.

Jean Walker has taught in Zimbabwe and in Britain and is now Deputy Director of the London Diocesan Board for Schools.

John White was for many years head of English at a London comprehensive school. He is now secretary of the Education Committee of the British Humanist Association.

Preface

The aim of these papers is not only to examine the provisions in the 1988 Education Reform Act with regard to religious education and worship in schools, but also to relate them to the historical situation that has produced them and to the educational and social situation in which they have to operate. The contributions of Josephine Cairns are concerned with assessing the extent to which the previous provisions, of the 1944 Education Act, were handicapped by the fact that they were not entirely suited to the culture of the time, and examines whether the new provisions are more realistic and likely to provide opportunities for a genuine education about beliefs and values. The chapters by Edwin Cox examine in detail the provisions of the 1988 Act which deal with religious education and school worship, pointing out their ambiguities and the problems their implementation will cause for pupils, teachers, parents and others involved.

The contributions to the Appendix were all written separately, and from a personal point of view, by individuals within certain of the main belief communities. It must be emphasized that they are not official pronouncements, representing the considered view of those communities (which would probably take a very different form), but cameos of the reactions of writers who have contact with education and who hold definite beliefs. They are influenced by the sharply differing reactions of the various life stances to the new requirements. That divergence of opinion should arise in them from time to time is, therefore, to be expected, and this draws attention to the imprecision of some of the clauses of the Act as witnessed to by the discussions, some of them controversial, that they are already provoking.

It is hoped that this volume, taken as a whole, will be regarded as an informed and judicious contribution to those discussions.

Chapter One
Introduction
Edwin Cox

In considering the religious provisions of the 1988 Education Reform Act it is necessary to take into account its relationship to the 1944 Education Act. The latter made worship and teaching about religion a legal requirement in British schools for the first time. The resulting education has not always been as successful as was hoped and cultural and ethnic changes in British society has made necessary reconsideration of the 1944 enactments. The recent 1988 Act aims to reinforce and clarify the existing provisions, as well as alter them to make them more applicable to the changed situation. It therefore supplements the 1944 Act rather than supersedes it, and an analysis of the legal status that religious education is to suffer or enjoy from now on has to refer to them together.

It is interesting to note that the first draft of the Bill which led to the 1988 Act made the briefest of references to religious education. It said much about other subjects which were to form the core of a new national curriculum, but it was unnecessary to include religious education in that core list because it was already a legal requirement as a result of the 1944 Act. Those who drafted the Bill either assumed that religious education was being effective and could remain unchanged or, knowing it to be a subject liable to arouse controversy and high feelings, thought it best not to bring it into the area of public educational debate. If it were the latter, a certain amount of unconcern might be inferred, but, in the light of the space eventually given to religious education in the revised form of the Bill, this inference would probably be ungenerous.

What emerged in that revision was a series of clauses which largely repeated the 1944 provisions, defined more precisely what was meant by them where there was uncertainty, stated in greater detail the extent of their application and where modifications and exceptions are permitted, and tried to make increased provision for the control and monitoring of the

1

subject. Consequently it is necessary to begin this critique of the 1988 Act and accompanying speculation about its intentions and likely consequences by a review of the major requirements of the 1944 Education Act.

Briefly, the chief enactments of 1944 were these:

1. In all schools the day was to begin with an act of collective worship attended by all pupils.
2. Religious instruction was to be given regularly to all pupils.
3. In all schools, other than those that were aided or special agreement schools, the instruction was normally to be according to an agreed syllabus.
4. Every local educational authority was to make an agreed syllabus or adopt one properly made by another authority.
5. Agreed syllabuses were to be made by an Agreed Syllabus Conference, consisting of four panels representing the Church of England, other religious denominations, the local authority and teachers' associations.
6. Parents had the right to ask that their children be withdrawn both from the worship and from the periods of instruction. Moreover they could, under certain conditions, ask that their children be given religious instruction different from that normally provided in the school (i.e. instruction according to the tenets of a particular religion when the school used an agreed syllabus, and instruction according to an agreed syllabus when the aided and special agreement schools gave denominational teaching).
7. No teacher in a maintained or controlled school could be required to take part in the worship or give the instruction in religion, or be in any way handicapped as a result of disinclination to do so.
8. An LEA might, if it wished, set up a Standing Advisory Council on Religious Education (SACRE) to help it discharge its duties under the Act.

In view of later developments it is interesting to notice what the 1944 Act omitted and what it left undefined. Although regular worship is required, nothing is said about what form it is to take and what material is to be used therein. Apart from providing that the syllabuses are to be what the mainly Christian panels of the Syllabus Conferences can agree about, the content of the instruction is not defined. It was, however, assumed that the Cowper-Temple clause still applied. That clause was an amendment to the 1870 Elementary Education Act, moved by a Liberal MP, W. F. Cowper-Temple, which provided that 'No religious catechism or formulary distinctive of any particular denomination shall be taught' in the newly established Board Schools. Apart from that negative stipulation, the government of the time, having willed religious instruction, apparently felt incapable of saying what was to be included in it, and passed this responsibility to the Syllabus Conferences, whom they envisaged would contain the religious experts and theologians capable of making the needed decisions. A minor omission which has since been used by those who oppose religious education, and those who have found it difficult with adolescents, is any statement as to whether the Act applies to all children in schools, irrespective of their ages, or only to those below the statutory school leaving age. The 1988 Act tries to be more specific on these matters.

Perhaps the most peculiar aspect of the 1944 Act is that, while stipulating religious education, which is to be composed of worship and religious instruction, it does not state which religion or religions are to be taught. It has been said that this was out of consideration for the few Jewish schools that then existed, but the reason is probably more subtle than that. Little being known in Britain at that time of other faiths, it was tacitly assumed that Christianity was the only faith that pupils were likely to encounter, the only faith about which they, therefore, need be educated, perhaps even the only faith that was worthy of study. One is confirmed in thinking this was so by the fact that no provision was made for Syllabus Conferences to include non-Christian representation. It seems to have been assumed that Christianity was the religion for Britain, that most people in the country would describe themselves as Christian, that the Christian ideals provided the foundation of 'the spiritual and personal values in our society and our national tradition'[1] and that the young would be able to respond to Christian teaching and thereby learn those personal, spiritual and national values.

Whether or not this was indeed the case, or whether it was assuming a national ethos that may possibly have pertained in the past but was not entirely applicable to 1944, is a matter of debate. Certainly it was not the done thing to criticize or to express doubts about Christian doctrine, and in moments of crisis in the Second World War, when Days of National Prayer were proclaimed, the Churches were full to the doors. But church attendance had declined steadily since the beginning of the century. There was a lingering guilt about this, and many expressed the regret that they 'could not find time to go to church'. What this meant was that other things had become more important to them, that Christianity had ceased to have prior hold on their affections, but that it had not yet become respectable to say so openly. There was perhaps a vague residual Christianity which showed itself in tolerance, kindliness and neighbourliness, but did not need for its expression a fully developed theological and liturgical system that regular attendance at Church provides. This is discussed more fully in Chapter 10 , but if it is an accurate description of the religious situation in 1944, the Act of that year was legislating for a society that had ceased to exist, and some of the difficulties that religious education has since encountered may have arisen from that fact. The situation has changed even more in the intervening years but unfortunately, in spite of that, the 1988 Education Reform Act seems to make the same assumptions – with a few minor concessions – and not only reinforces the provisions of the earlier act, but also defines them more precisely to apply to a culture that is taken to be in general, still predominantly Christian.

Reference

1 Board of Education (1943) *Educational Reconstruction*. London: HMSO.

Chapter Two
Religious Education and the 1944 Education Act: Missed Opportunities
Josephine M. Cairns

In 1938 the Spens Report argued:

> No boy or girl can be counted as properly educated unless he or she has been made aware of the fact of the existence of a religious interpretation of life.[1]

In spite of religious education not being a legally required part of the curriculum at that time, the schools were urged, even at an official level, to educate their pupils about religion. This was not altogether surprising since even those new phenomena of the industrial age, the Mass-Observation polls, pointed up the obvious place of religion within the experience of the majority of the population. For instance, in a poll of 1938 which asked what factors contributed most to a person's happiness religion was ranked third of ten. Yet T. S. Eliot at the same time was able to say in *The Rock*

> In the land of lobelias and tennis flannels
> The rabbits shall burrow and the thorn revisit
> The nettle shall flourish on the gravel court,
> And the wind shall say: Here were decent godless people.[2]

The fact was that religion already occupied that ambiguous place in the social, political and personal lives of the British which it still does today. Religious clauses in the 1988 Act which beg so many questions are the direct result.

The Church and society: different perspectives
Notwithstanding this ambiguity, orthodox religion was being advocated for inclusion in the school curriculum before the war. The Cambridgeshire

syllabus of 1939, which provided the model for syllabus development required by the 1944 Act, offers an excellent example. It introduces its readers to a sensitive and clear analysis of the problems facing the country at the time, while prescribing a specific treatment of Christianity as the remedy for social and political ills.

> The most menacing thing about our civilization is its lack of direction...ancient certainties by which our fathers lived and died seem irrelevant and almost meaningless to the children who have to live from crisis to crisis. Incertitude is the mark of the hour.
>
> Our problem, though so acute today, is really very old. It springs out of the old truth that the only Gospel by which men can live must be a big and positive thing. Unless it can build up and sustain the organic unity of human life at all levels, it is no Gospel at all.[3]

Many commentators of the time seem to agree with this analysis of the personal and social problems facing Britain. As will be shown later, not all of them agreed with the evangelistic nature of the remedy that the Cambridge syllabus proposed:

> Christian teaching is one of the highest and specialized privileges of Christian discipleship and whenever it is going forward the classroom becomes a place that is 'Holy unto the Lord' and its fellowship a miniature realization of the fellowship of the Church.[3]

To describe briefly society as it then was, we need to explain the diversity in life style and political affiliation which characterized pre-war Britain. For some in that society there had been no relief from depression, unemployment and hunger since the end of the First World War; yet for others this had been a time of opportunity in the new light industries and the service and entertainment trades. In Coventry, for example, which had become the home of the car industry, there was only five per cent unemployment in 1934, whereas in Jarrow 68 per cent of the community had no work. J. B. Priestley in his *English Journey*, published in 1934, commented:

> Every future historian of modern England should be compelled to take a good, long, slow walk around Gateshead. After that he can at his leisure fit it into his interpretation of our national growth and development.[4]

One part of society, then, was rejoicing in its new found material prosperity and looked to the government to ensure its continuance, while another part sought to express its frustration and anger through political and trades union activities in opposition to the established ruling groups. This was the tense and complex situation in which education sought to serve the needs of the community. In 1929, for example, Stanley Baldwin wrote a letter to teachers which contained the following advice:

> The classification of our schools has been on the lines of social rather than educational distinction; a youth's school badge has been his social label. The interests of social unity demand the removal of this source of class prejudice and the drastic remodelling of the national structure to form a coherent whole.[5]

These were not the only changes afoot in Britain at the time. On the one hand there were pronounced differences between living in the north or the south of the country, between attending a grammar school or an elementary school, between living in the Welsh valleys or the Midlands, but, on the other hand, the development of the means of communication and the fact that virtually the whole population could read helped to mitigate divisions. The popular press grew and made people conscious of their national leaders and the presence of an international world. The wireless and the cinemas brought the news into the lives of the majority of the people as it was taking place; so too the cinema portrayed the luxury and deprivation of the United States. In these ways the community could now be said to be sharing common experiences to an extent and a depth which was previously unknown.

Education for peace: individualism versus cohesion
The war intensified the sense of a community sharing common experiences. Thus, in extending the education service more widely across the community, the government in 1944 was faced not only with shaping an education adequate to meet these changes but one which might help to restructure a nation after the exhaustion and confusion of war. A war must necessarily call into question the values held in common or individually; and the need to help the young find their place in an educated democracy was urgent. It is to the direction of education in the war-torn atmosphere of the early 1940s that we must now turn, since the debates of that time help to explain the 1944 Education Act. In particular we must examine the role which was envisaged for religious education within the scope of those debates and the role which religious education then found for itself.

On 17 February 1942 William Temple, Archbishop of Canterbury and proponent of Christian socialism, spoke in the House of Lords during a debate on the future of education. He argued that:

It is certainly vain to think that a great democracy can wisely meet the problems that will confront the nation, and indeed the world, when this tremendous struggle has been brought to a victorious end, unless it is in the truest sense of the word an educated democracy.

The government and those involved in education put stress on the growth of the individual as central to the new endeavours of education. This idea was expressed in section 36 of the 1944 Act:

It shall be the duty of the parent of every child of compulsory school age to cause him to receive efficient full-time education suitable for his age, ability and aptitude.[6]

The White Paper, *Educational Reconstruction* published in 1943, had made clear the desire to improve the individual lives of the young:

The government's purpose in putting forward the reforms...is to secure for children a happier childhood and a better start in life...and to provide means for all of developing the various talents with which they are endowed and so enriching the inheritance of the country whose citizens they are.[7]

In such ways the government switched educational activity away from a former emphasis on purely vocational training for the good of society to a concern for the development of the individual child to his or her full potential. The way was thus prepared for a growth in self-consciousness but not necessarily in community consciousness.

There were voices that expressed concern at the time. In August and September of 1942 the *Times Educational Supplement* published a series of articles under the title 'What is Religious Education?'[8] The articles were written by H. A. Hamilton, a Congregationalist Minister and at one time Principal of Westhill College, Selly Oak, Birmingham, and they received the following comment in an editorial:

There was never more need than today for a searching examination of values upon which our lives as individuals and our life as a people should be based. In the end, Mr Hamilton says, 'religion depends on the conscious direction of the personality by the will.' The same applies to the collective personality of the community. The British personality retains all its force and charm; but today it is sadly misdirected.[9]

Religious education: an ecclesiastical or secular duty?
Thus the work of imposing a collective consciousness was laid on the shoulders of religious education. To this end the advice of Hamilton in one of his articles was valuable because he argues that religion is

a conviction about the nature of reality by which a man is prepared to live. It will direct his choice and guide his purpose...thus we are concerned to prepare them (the pupils) for life, to train their capacity for relationships, to give them a sense of values about what is worth seeking.[8]

With such a clear definition of religion to form the basis for the work of religious education, it is appropriate to speculate what problems it left unsolved for the subject, for it presumed:

1. That lessons in religion provide the setting for reflection and discussion about relationships and values, even among pupils whose attitudes and beliefs in this area may not have resulted from conscious religious beliefs.
2. That religious education is an appropriate channel for the dissemination of attitudes and values to all young people at whatever stage of their development.
3. That the Christian experience of truth is all-pervasive and that this Christian experience is open to all in an educational setting.

This perspective on the role of religious education at the time is also reflected in the words of Basil Yeaxlee speaking to a conference of teachers in 1942:

As the child grew up he began to ask for the meaning of all he had learned; religious teaching was the key which would help him carry forward to a community which was a family, which was democratic, in which all sought the good of others, because all were children of one Father.[10]

The aim of religious education can thus broadly be defined at this time as to enable the young person to find meaning in experience as a result of embracing the values of Christianity. For Christian educators there was no problem here: they assumed that all would respond to the values of Christianity since their own belief led them to see all human beings as children of the one Christian God. We must therefore examine the question whether the 1944 Education Act set the appropriate conditions for the religious educators of the time to test their theory that all children could be helped to see the validity of Christian truth.

In so far as the Act provided, first, that the main focus of religious education was to be a collective act of worship and, second, that instruction was to be given according to an agreed syllabus which was to contain materials that the Christian denominations could agree about, the signs were propitious for the provision of a successful Christian education.

Its support for a Christian approach to the process of religious education was further strengthened by the composition of the Agreed Syllabus Conferences, which were designed to contain predominant proportions of Christian representatives. The conditions may have been propitious but legislation could not ensure that the outcome would necessarily meet the needs for which it had been designed.

In the first place members of Syllabus Conferences were largely chosen from those who had only distant contact with the classroom and who saw Christianity in a strongly doctrinal, ecclesiastical and Biblical light. Secondly, as has already been noted, the background needs of the pupils had changed as a result of a variety of factors, primarily, at this stage, the need to adjust to living and planning in a depressed and chaotic post-war world. That need was indeed taken into account by the White Paper preceding the 1944 Act, which called upon the schools and religious education in particular, 'to revive the personal and spiritual values of the nation'.[7] It might have been met if proper recognition had been given to the serious moral and religious strivings involved in the pupils' experiences and which underlay the questions which they brought into the classroom. Unfortunately the teaching that resulted from the agreed syllabuses confined the boundaries of religious thinking to Biblical knowledge and ecclesiastical history, thus preventing the pupils from meeting with Christian thinking at the point where it impinged upon personal and social problems and questions of value. Thus, though the Act allowed for a Christian education which might have been acceptable and effective in taking seriously the personal and social development of the pupils of the time, the religious education that was actually provided proved a mismatch with the reality of the classroom and the intentions of the legislators.

Post-Christian secularism: an opportunity?
Nevertheless, some of the guidelines which the syllabuses offered merit attention, in that they point to ways in which the Act might have proved fruitful in the areas of moral and spiritual growth. In the first place they remind the teacher that the ultimate aim of religious education 'is not to get over to the child a body of facts but to inculcate and foster a comprehensible way of life'.[11] In other words the pupils should be enabled to discern the values and philosophy behind the life style which they adopt as their own. Some of the syllabuses suggest means by which this might be achieved: an intitiation of the pupils into ways in which their culture has previously tackled problems similar to those they themselves encountered; an encouragement of the pupils to seek principles which would help

them find purpose and meaning in their lives; and an imparting of an impetus to maintain these principles and to follow them for the greater social good. Such a model for working in the area of personal and spiritual development in the classrooms of a post-war country contains exciting potential, but to be effective the application of that model has to be on a base broad enough not to exclude any particular pupil group. In fact the syllabuses linked the model with a restrictive Biblical and ecclesiastical study which could only include in its scope those pupils whose attitudes were already favourably disposed to a formal and organized Christianity. For instance the Surrey syllabus of 1945 says:

> The aim of the syllabus is to secure that children...may find inspiration, power and courage to work for their own welfare, for that of their fellow creatures, and for the growth of God's kingdom.[12]

The syllabus divided its content into two sections entitled 'The Bible and its Teaching' and 'The Christian Life'.

It would appear in retrospect that the religious temper of the time was not so ecclesiastically Christian. Rather it was a mixture of the Christian idea of providence and pragmatic humanism; what has since come to be called 'residual' Christianity. Instead of attempting a methodical Christian indoctrination it might have been wiser for religious educators to pay heed to the advice offered them in a *Times Educational Supplement* leader in October 1943:

> As it is by no means certain yet that the basic philosophy of England will be in the future a Christian philosophy – which not unimportant sections of the community consciously and deliberately reject – any attempt to capture the schools for the systematic inculcation of the Christian view of life would be wrong and might well precipitate embittered conflict between rival religious and political parties for possession of the schools.[8]

The way would then have been clear for all young people in this increasingly educated democracy to participate in worthwhile classroom debate about the relation between their own attitudes, values and spiritual perceptions and those of the community as a whole.

Articulating and challenging the values of post-Christian secularism: an opportunity missed

What remains problematic about the legislation concerning religious education in the 1944 Act is the provision for a corporate act of worship.

Many commentators at the time pointed out the need for some serious investigation in schools of the community's values, and some systematic inculcation of values in the young. Few of them, however, could support the validity of a compulsory act of worship in the nation's schools. The act of worship stood little chance of creating positive and sincere responses in the pupils unless it had the whole-hearted support and encouragement of the general population, which it did not in fact enjoy. Once again the overriding ecclesiastical influence on religion in schools following the 1944 Act had prevented the schools taking the opportunities of promoting and celebrating those aspects of experience which the community found worthy and valuable. A narrowly conceived religious education was thought to be providing an adequate celebration of the national aspirations and values, while it was in fact preventing something more genuinely related to the community's perceptions from being developed.

It can be argued, then, that the educational system failed the newly emerging culture by not allowing its values to become conscious and to be expressed and celebrated. Had those opportunities been taken there might have arisen an educated post-Christian democracy, conscious of its values, instead of one which grows confused, turbulent and increasingly aggressive. A foundation might then have been laid for a reasoned and purposeful pluralism to take shape in the rapidly changing post-war community. The aims of the 1944 Act in religious education have not been wholly realized and the 1988 Act, in its own way, has to do the work over again. Whether its provisions are sufficiently sensitive to the reality of the situation, and whether they will prove to be more effective, remains to be seen.

References

1 Board of Education (1938) *Secondary Education with Special Reference to Grammar Schools and Technical High Schools* (The Spens Report). London: HMSO.

2 Eliot, T. S. (1934) *The Rock*. London: Faber & Faber.

3 Cambridgeshire Syllabus of Religious Teaching for Schools (revised edition, 1939).

4 Priestley, J. B. (1934) *English Journey*. Harmondsworth: Penguin Books (1987 edition).

5 Baldwin, Stanley, quoted in Eaglesham, E. J. R. (second edition, 1972) *The Foundations of 20th Century Education in England*. London: Routledge & Kegan Paul.

6 Education Act 1944, Section 36. London: HMSO.

7 Board of Education (1943) *Educational Reconstruction*. London: HMSO.

8 Hamilton, H. A. 'What is Religious Education?' *Times Educational Supplement* (18 November, 1942). London.

9 *Times Educational Supplement* (30 October, 1943). London.

10 Yeaxlee, Basil, quoted in *Religion in Education* (Vol. 9, No.4, October, 1942). London: SCM Press.

11 London Agreed Syllabus: London County Council Agreed Syllabus, 1947.

12 Surrey Agreed Syllabus, 1945.

Chapter Three
The Years Between
Edwin Cox

Since 1944 neither the cultural scene in Britain nor the religious education undertaken in its schools have remained static. There have been changes in the ethnic composition of the country, in educational theory and practice, in theological and in moral thinking, and in attitudes to religions. Religious education could not be unaffected by those changes and it has been modified from time to time to meet the changed situation and retain its credibility. Not everyone has welcomed changes in the subject, nor understood the reasons for them, and this has led to diversity in the teaching and sometimes to a worried misunderstanding on the part of religious leaders and legislators of what teachers were trying to do. The debates that preceded the 1988 Act tended to reflect that anxious concern. Before it is possible to assess how far the new Act has adequately taken into account those changes it is necessary to recount briefly what the changes were and the manner in which religious education has responded to them.

A failure to communicate
The first pressure for a consideration of possible modification in the way the subject was handled in schools came from tensions within the religious education provisions themselves. Towards the end of the 1950s it was realized that the teaching was not having the effect that had been hoped. The young showed no greater inclination to react to the Christian basis of British personal and national values or even to see the connection between those values and what was taught about religion in the classroom. Rather, church-going was declining among young people, juvenile delinquency increasing, and a disrespect for authority and traditional forms of culture becoming evident. Conscientiously taught, religious education was not meeting pupils' needs or interests and having scant effect on their outlook

and behaviour. Moreover they were becoming restlessly critical of it and of the school worship they were expected to attend. A number of reports produced at this time[1] showed that though pupils were concerned with the issues that religious education sought to raise, they were finding little help in the teaching that was actually being given, which either did not seem to them to relate closely to the issues or to discuss them in a form that the pupils could understand. The content of the religious education lesson seemed irrelevant to their lives and concerns and consequently they were remembering little of what was being taught and misunderstanding a good deal of the little they were remembering[2].

The cause of this failure of communication probably lay in the nature of the provisions for religious education. The legislators may have been right in thinking that the basic religion of the country was still Christianity, and there was strong support in the population that children should be given the opportunity in schools of learning what Christianity was about, but what most understood by Christianity was not a highly theological, sacramental, Bible-based religion, but something more generalized, a kind of folk faith, a respect for the main Christian ethical tenets, which involved generosity, kindliness, tolerance and decent neighbourliness, but had little use for careful doctrinal definitions, for the minutiae of liturgical procedure, or for delving into the intricacies of Biblical scholarship. But as already noted, Parliament had handed over the decisions of what precisely should be taught to Local Authority Syllabus Conferences, who, in the early days, contained a high proportion of distinguished Church leaders and eminent theologians, whose opinions were treated with respect by members of the LEA and teacher association panels. These Christian dignitaries and scholars were not concerned with a folk faith, but with the finer and more detailed points of doctrine, worship and Biblical scholarship.

Furthermore the Conferences were charged with making syllabuses that would be acceptable to all the main Christian Protestant denominations, who were more divided than they are now, but were agreed that the Bible is a sacred book and that Bible study is desirable. They found it easy to subscribe to schemes of Bible study. As a result the early syllabuses tended to be dominated by study of the Christian scriptures and to be based on assumptions that were more doctrinal and ecclesiastical than were acceptable to a folk faith. This may be the reason why the religious education that resulted from them was remote from the interests of the pupils and consequently inclined to be ineffective. Once that ineffectiveness had been recognized, as a result of the researches of the late 1950s, there began a series of attempts to make religious education more relevant to the views of the pupils, which have been going on ever since.

Educational changes

It was at about the same time that new ideas of educational practice began to influence the subject. The general retreat from authoritarianism began to appear in educational theory. No longer was teaching seen as the transmission of knowledge which the teachers had and which the pupils accepted on their authority; rather it was to be 'inductive', which meant that pupils were to be guided by the teachers to experiment and discover for themselves what there is to be known. If other subjects used this method religious education would be forced to follow their lead. This created something of a problem because religions do not take all that kindly to inductive learning. They believe in revealed truths that are accepted on authority and with humility; faithful acceptance can be regarded as preferable to finding out for oneself, which can be looked on with reservation, or as dangerous, because it could lead to individual heretical ideas. Nonetheless religious education began in the 1960s to take on an inductive tinge, which made possible the 'implicit religion approach'[3] of the later years of the decade.

Changes in psychological and theological understanding

An even greater influence for change was the fresh insight into the way that growing children react to and understand religious ideas, which came as a result of the researches of R J Goldman[4], K E Hyde[5] and others published between 1964 and 1967. The gist of their findings was that religious thinking follows the pattern of thinking described by Piaget, proceeding from pre-operational thinking, through concrete thinking, to abstract thinking in adolescence. Until they reach the final abstract thinking stage children are usually incapable of understanding fully the subtler meta-phorical and symbolic forms in which religious statements are couched; instead they think of them firstly in a confused way and then concretely and literally, consequently misunderstanding them and having too simplistic an idea of what religion is about. This causes them to find in early adolescence that their religious ideas conflict with the logico-scientific view of reality that they are acquiring in their other studies, so that many of them reject religion as 'childish' and never achieve the ability to think abstractly about it.

The research raised two questions about the conduct of religious education: firstly whether teaching about those aspects of religion involving abstract thinking for full apprehension was appropriate at all in the primary school, since it was likely eventually to give misleading ideas and so to be counter-productive; secondly whether teaching in the secondary school was helping pupils to deepen and refine their ideas about religion and see a relationship between it and other ways of viewing experience. Was it not rather confirming their literalistic ideas, whereas a more open and questioning approach might help them think maturely about religion now that they had the mental capacity to do so? What changes in the approach to the subject were needed?

Strangely, part of the answer to that question came from certain developments in theological thinking. These had been going on for some time but had been confined to the thinking of theological scholars and had not influenced the average churchgoer, much less the non-churchgoing population. They suddenly became widely known and discussed as the result of the publication of John Robinson's *Honest to God*[6] in 1963. This book made available in popular form ideas that were to be found in the writings of such men as Bultmann, Tillich and Bonhoeffer, who had noted that the scientific and philosophical knowledge that the human race had acquired during the past three centuries made belief in God, as expressed in the traditional formulations, difficult for modern men and women to accept. The idea of a God as an entity that maintained a quasi-physical relationship with the created world, as was implied by many of the myths and miracles stories that religions treasured, was no longer plausible. So what did the term 'God' mean? Bultmann had observed that God was to 'be found in the natural not in the unnatural'[7], and Tillich had said that God was to be found 'in the depth and ground of being'[8] and that religion was 'what you took seriously without reservation'. The effect of this was to reduce the authoritarian element in Christian theology and to allow a certain amount of personal search in the pursuit of religious truth. Religion had become a more flexible and a more personal thing, no longer a confident proclamation of indisputable revealed truth, but rather a search for truth through the interpretation of experience.

The new theology, as it was called, had two immediate effects on religious education. In the first instance, it appeared to remove from the subject some of its content and to cast doubts on its traditionally dogmatic and confessionally based presentation; in the second instance, it made the subject more amenable to an inductive treatment, making it an open search for meaning in life. The way was shown by Harold Loukes who viewed the whole of education as a dialogue with experience to discover its significance. For Loukes, religious education was to start not from revelations and doctrines but from personal experience which was to be looked at in depth to discover the religious significance therein. Conducted by means of life themes and discussions, this way of treating the subject became known as 'the implicit religion approach'[3]. It was widely used by teachers in the late 1960s but survived for only a short time. There were two reasons for its brevity: the first was that it did not seem to touch pupils' imagination and to affect them any more than the older religious education had done – possibly looking at life in depth needed more sophistication than most children could bring to it; secondly a new social factor had come to bear on the situation which necessitated a further rethinking of what kind of religious education was appropriate for Britain in the closing decades of the twentieth century.

The coming of religious pluralism

Until 1965 it was still possible to retain the impression that Christianity was the only influential religion in Britain and the only one that needed to be dealt with extensively in religious education. Immigrants had been arriving for some time, but by now they were sufficiently numerous to make their presence felt. Groups could be found in several large cities who were practising other religions, acquiring facilities for worship and wishing their children to be brought up in the family faith. Furthermore the increase in foreign travel meant that Britons were coming into contact with those religions in their indigenous settings. Those religions suddenly seemed to have ideas which were not so erroneous as had been thought and appeared to have the right to be respected as genuine alternatives to Christianity. Thoughts of that nature compelled reconsideration of the mainly Christian content of the agreed syllabuses. Was that sufficient or did the changed situation and view demand that, in the pursuit of truth and in deference to the other religious groups now found in the country, its borders be enlarged to take in other respectable faiths?

The immigrant children posed particular problems in schools. Were they to be taught Christianity like the others as part of their enculturizing process, or were they to be educated in the faiths which were being practised in their homes? What is more, was there not needed some inter-faith education, so that the more or less Christian native population could understand and sympathize with the religious beliefs and practices of their new schoolfellows, and so that the followers of the newly arrived religions could understand each other and the indigenous Christian population? Though teaching about religions other than Christianity was not officially recognized in any agreed syllabus until that of Birmingham in 1975, many schools were responding to the new religious pluralism and teaching about world faiths from about 1970 or earlier.

The new approach to religious education affected not only the content of the lessons but also the attitude to religion and the teaching of it. All religions were to be respected as being valid, and as seeming to have truth in them if looked at from the point of view of the believer. From this it followed that none of them could be regarded as the norm by which others were to be assessed, so the question of ultimate truth in religion could not be raised. The study of them was, therefore, to be 'phenomenological'. The object of phenomenological study is to try and understand what a religion means to an adherent, to see it through the eyes of a believer and to sympathize with how a believer feels when being religious. The question of whether the believer is right or wrong in so believing and feeling is not raised, and it is axiomatic that 'the believer is always right'.

This type of religious education, known as phenomenological[9], or as 'the explicit religion approach'[3] has been widely used in the 1970s and 1980s and has been strongly influential in shaping the aims and objectives of the agreed syllabuses produced during that time, but there are reservations about it. Failing to take into account the truth claims of religions has two consequences. Practically it means that the teaching is confined to the externals of religions, their places of worship, their cult objects and their festivals. Their deeper beliefs which justify those places, objects and festivals are carefully avoided in case they raise truth claims. Such teaching can give the impression that religion is a superficial set of customs practised by those who happen to like them. More profoundly the avoidance of truth claims can suggest that no type of religion can have any deep significance, or lead to truth, and therefore that religious education is not an imperative study, and can be indoctrination into agnosticism. Insensitively presented 'explicit' teaching can result in a trivializing of religion. Further, it is debatable how far younger children (or early adolescents for that matter) have the subtlety and sophistication to try and put themselves in another's place and not be concerned with whether those persons are right or wrong in their beliefs. They are more likely to pose the question 'Well is it true?', and if they are prevented from asking that question the study is not going to influence the critical development of their own beliefs.

Though it was orthodox to say that one's religious education was phenomenological, not all teachers who claimed to use that method were observing the strict canons of phenomenology. They began with giving information about the externals of religion but went on, often because they were forced to by pupils' questions, to discuss the ideas that lay behind religious practices with the view of imparting a deeper understanding of them and appealing to pupils' own experience in evoking that understanding. What such teachers were doing was to employ both the implicit and the explicit approaches as appropriate to pupils' interests and needs, and teaching that was both helpful and acceptable to the pupils often followed. That perceptive teachers were so forced to abandon strict phenomonology in the interest of pupil understanding may indicate that, useful though the method may be in theological study, it has its drawbacks in the school classroom. It is possible that an objective, non-judgemental, strictly explicit and phenomenological religious education is not giving pupils enough help in working out their own sincere belief systems and that the implicit religion approach was abandoned too soon and might usefully be revived. Maybe a mixture of implicit and explicit study is needed so that the teaching becomes both 'a dialogue with religions' and 'a dialogue with experience'[10].

A wider pluralism?
In developing the study of world religions, religious education has tried to adapt to religious pluralism but that may not mean that it need contemplate no further change because it is perfectly suited to the present social and intellectual situation. There is religious pluralism, but that may be but part of a more complex pluralism.

Alongside the religious believers there are considerable numbers who hold to belief systems that cannot strictly be called religious. Some are not without sympathy for a religious point of view but are indifferent to all forms of organized religions; they have a residual folk faith, which has no need of theology or ecclesiasticism, and which is not strong enough deeply to influence their life styles, which are for the most part secular. There are an increasing number who are agnostic, some who have embraced one of the life stances which share 'many of the dimensions of religion whilst not admitting belief in realities that transcend the natural order'[11], and some who class themselves as thoroughly materialist and agnostic. The effect is that alongside our religious pluralism there is another pluralism which is fundamentally secular, and in understanding the culture both pluralisms have to be taken into account.

This raises the question of whether a school subject that deals with the religious hemisphere and ignores the secular hemisphere is a justifiable part of the educational system. Is the religious hemisphere large enough for it to be made the basis of a school subject by itself? By teaching about religions it is catering for those who belong to one of them, and perhaps giving some understanding of them to those who do not belong, but is it doing anything to assist the development of those children who come from homes that are attached to no religion and doubtful about the efficacy of all of them? Or ought it to enlarge its borders yet further and become part of a study of how men and women derive their values and their life styles from their fundamental beliefs, be they theistic or non-theistic? In other words, having in the past 20 years come to terms with religious pluralism, should religious education try to comprehend the secular pluralism as well?

Official publications have been feeling their way towards this further extending of horizons. *A Framework for the School Curriculum* (1980) spoke of it being right 'for religious education to be linked with the wider consideration of personal and social values'[12]. *The School Curriculum* (1981) said 'it forms part of the curriculum's concern for personal and social values'[13]. One would have expected such views to have influenced the religious clauses of the 1988 Education Reform Act but they do not appear to have done so.

Changes such as have been discussed in this chapter have radically altered the face of society and its schools, where teaching and learning are by no means the same as they were in 1944. Religious education has responded partially to those changes and may need still further modification. Assessment of the likely effects of the religious provisions of the 1988 Act will involve enquiring into how far those who drew it up have accepted changes in the subject as valid reactions to the changing society and how far their Act will help the subject to be sensitive to further need for adaption. Reading the Act it is easy to get the impression that the government has not been much influenced by the changes that have occurred since 1944, but have been content to repeat and strengthen the religious clauses of the earlier Act, while making some allowance for the coming of religious pluralism. It remains to be seen how far the religious education that is envisaged and legally required is realistic and apt for British society as it is now.

References

1 e.g. Institute of Christian Education (1957), *Religious Education in Schools*. London: SPCK; University of Sheffield (1961), *Religious Education in Secondary Schools*. London: Nelson.

2 Loukes, H. (1961), *Teenage Religion*. London: SCM Press; Cox, E. (1967), *Sixth Form Religion*. London: SCM Press.

3 The term was first used in Schools Council (1971), *Religious Education in Secondary Schools* (Working Paper 36). London: Evans Bros.

4   Goldman, R. J. (1964), *Religious Thinking from Childhood to Adolescence*. London: Routledge and Kegan Paul.

5   Hyde, K.E. (1965), *Religious Learning in Adolescence*. Birmingham: University of Birmingham Institute of Education.

6   Robinson, J. A. T. (1963), *Honest to God*. London: SCM Press.

7   Bultmann, R. (1958), *Jesus Christ and Mythology*. New York: Scribner.

8   Tillich, P. (1962), *The Shaking of the Foundations*. Harmondsworth, Middlesex: Penguin Books.

9   See Sharpe, E. (1975), 'The phenomenology of religion', *Learning for Living* 15,1 (Autumn). London: SCM Press.

10 Schools Council (1977), *A Groundplan for the Study of Religion*. London: Schools Council.

11 Birmingham Agreed Syllabus, 1975.

12 Department of Education and Science (1980), *A Framework for the School Curriculum*. London: HMSO.

13 Department of Education and Science (1981), *The School Curriculum*. London: HMSO.

Chapter Four
Agreed Syllabuses
Education Reform Act 1988, Sections 8 and Schedule 1
Edwin Cox

Britain, unlike certain other countries, has never had a closely defined curriculum for its schools. The requirements of examining bodies and the inner logic of subjects being taught have had some influence on what has been included in lessons, but on the whole decisions about what to include and what not to include in syllabuses has been left to the good sense of heads and subject teachers, influenced perhaps by governing bodies. Religious education alone has been required to keep to a defined syllabus, but even then a syllabus decided locally rather than nationally.

Recently, new notions about the nature of academic subjects and new theories about teaching methods, often imaginative but not always deeply thought out, have led to an unease about what is being taught in schools. This has been exacerbated by feelings that teachers are not entirely using their former good sense and that the curriculum needs firmer control to ensure that it is adequate and reflects the real educational and vocational needs of children in a technological age. One of the reforms that the 1988 Educational Reform Act is intended to initiate is a closer control of the curriculum at a national level. For reasons not entirely clear, however, religious education is not to be subjected to such central direction.

Religious education: a basic subject but not nationally defined
The Act divides school subjects into three categories: core subjects (mathematics, English, science), foundation subjects (history, geography, technology, music, art, physical education) and basic subjects (unspecified except for religious education). With the core and foundation subjects the Secretary of State is empowered to specify content of study, attainment

targets and arrangements for assessing the extent to which the targets are being attained. To guide him in this a National Curriculum Council, presumably with sub-committees of experts dealing with separate subjects, will be established. The result will be a national curriculum and national tests for core and foundation subjects, which will be used without much variation in all schools, promoting greater uniformity of practice and increased public centralized control over education in maintained schools.[1]

Although a basic subject, rather than a core or foundation one, religious education is officially considered to have similar status to other school subjects. This is made explicit in DES Circular 3/89 in the following terms:

> The special status of religious education as a part of the basic but not the National Curriculum is important. It ensures that religious education has equal standing in relation to the core and other foundation subjects within a school's curriculum, but is not subject to *nationally prescribed* attainment targets, programmes of study and assessment arrangements.[2]

If religious education is an essential part of education, sufficiently important to be mentioned on its own, and before the other subjects, in Clause 2 (1) (a) in the Act, one has to wonder why it is not to be given a national curriculum, but left, as before, to the decisions of local authorities and its content decided by local agreed syllabuses. This may be due to inertia, or to the feeling that the existing syllabuses, many of them carefully revised in the last few years and not all that radically different from one another, will suffice and there is no need to go to the trouble and expense of fashioning a national one. It may be thought that, since religion is a sensitive matter and has occasioned acute dissension in the past, to allow local interested parties to have a say in its definition will lead to less dispute, and that, because of the high feeling that religious education can evoke, the chances of agreement on a national syllabus are remote. It may be that for all its lip service to religious education, the government (or individual members of it) does not really think religious education is an inescapable part of school, but a troublesome ingredient that is best left to its own local devices.

More subtle and serious reasons, however, come to mind. Though governments have passed acts demanding that religion be included in the school curriculum they have hesitated to take the responsibility of saying precisely how it is to be treated, possibly from a feeling that they have not the expertise to do so. They have handed over that responsibility to those concerned with religion and asked them to decide, through their representation on Agreed Syllabus Conferences, what they would like taught. It is an interesting fact that when the government needs advice on religious education it turns first to leaders of religious bodies and not to the educators who are actually teaching and thinking about it, who are only asked to comment on what has been decided in the light of the advice received. Perhaps this perceived need to entrust the subject to religious experts inhibited the Secretary of State from claiming the right to specify content, targets and assessment tests for it.

Yet it would still have been possible to convene a sub-committee of the National Curriculum Council which included religious leaders and theologians. Why is religious education alone left to local control? The assumption behind this provision would seem to be that the teaching about religion has to be dealt with differently in different localities and that a common national syllabus would not meet pupils' needs. If this is the case it throws an interesting light on what Parliament thinks religious education is designed to accomplish. It is to teach mainly about the religion and the religious concerns of the neighbourhood, and be fashioned and monitored, to some extent, by local religious interests. Behind it is the hope that religious education will incline pupils to accept the predominant faith of the locality and so be welded into the local community. This opinion is reinforced by the fact that one of the panels of both Syllabus Conferences and Standing Advisory councils is to reflect the principal religious traditions in the area. How this will square with the stipulation that the syllabus shall reflect mainly the Christian tradition in areas where other religious faiths predominate is not clear. Possibly it is thought that such areas form a smallish part of Britain so that teaching there about other religions is appropriate and can be tolerated because it will not affect the Christian ethos of the country as a whole. There appears to be some confusion of thought here, which is discussed more fully below.

1988 modification of syllabus legislation

Teaching about religion in all maintained and controlled schools is to be according to an agreed syllabus. The rules for drawing up syllabuses and for the extent of their use are the same as those defined in the fifth schedule of the 1944 Act as modified in the first schedule of the 1988 Act. The former Act made it compulsory for every LEA to draw up its own syllabus, by means of a properly constituted Agreed Syllabus Conference or to adopt one so drawn up by another authority. This still pertains, but there are four notable modifications.

The first modification is a terminological one. The 1944 Act, when referring to classroom teaching about religion, used the term 'religious

instruction' and the syllabuses were legally referred to as syllabuses of
'religious instruction'. Much has been made of this, perhaps too much, by
commentators who have taken it to mean that this implied that the
teaching was to be authoritarian and indoctrinatory. The 1944 Act used
the term 'religious education', but meant it to refer both to the worship and
the classroom teaching and therefore had to find another term for the
classroom activity. Over the years teachers and others have fought shy of
using the word 'instruction' and the term 'religious education' has become
part of the accepted terminology. The new Act recognizes this and
substitutes the word 'education' for 'instruction' on every occasion.
Whether this implies a modified view of the nature of the subject or is a
concession to current educational linguistic fashion is worthy of
discussion.

The second modification is to the constitution of the Agreed Syllabus
Conferences. Three of their four panels remain unchanged (Church of
England, Local Authority and Teachers' Associations) but the fourth one,
which previously covered 'other religious denominations', has been
extended to include 'such Christian and other religious denominations as,
in the opinion of the authority, will appropriately reflect the principal
religious traditions of the area'[3]. In the past this panel has usually consisted
of Protestant Christian denominations, since the Roman Catholic Christians chose not to participate. The Birmingham Agreed Syllabus Conference of the early 1970s interpreted the description of this panel as
permitting the inclusion of members of non-Christian faiths found in the
vicinity. Now such persons will have a right to be represented on this panel
provided their religion has an adequate presence in the area. This could
mean that Syllabus Conferences will differ in their religious constitution
from place to place. Those of places such as Brent, Smethwick and
Bradford will have a much stronger non-Christian representation than
those of rural parts of England and Wales, though, with the Church of
England having a panel all to itself there will probably always be a strong
Christian presence. Some areas may have little or no representation of
other world religions, and this will be regarded as unfortunate by those
who think that religious education should prepare pupils to understand
and respect those religions that contribute widely to world culture and
which are likely to be encountered when pupils travel beyond their
immediate environment. An argument can be found for including
representatives of a multiplicity of religions on all Syllabus Conferences,
irrespective of their local influence.

The third modification is that the residual influence of the Cowper-
Temple clause has been slightly modified. Syllabuses still may not contain

catechisms or formulae distinctive of any religious denomination but they may now include the study of such denominational teaching[4]. Presumably this refers to the manner of the teaching rather than the matter. It is legal to teach that such and such a group believes certain things, or even takes certain things to be true, but illegal to imply or suggest that such things are true. This is somewhat ingenious and shows little appreciation either of the chemistry of the classroom or of up-to-date inductive teaching methods. Few teachers outside Church or religious schools expect pupils to accept beliefs as true without critical discussion, and this would be the case when studying denominational formulae. In those discussions intelligent pupils will accept as probably true those portions of the study which seem to them to relate to their experience and prior assumptions, and reject as false those portions that do not. They do not accept catechisms and formulae uncritically and unexamined, but study of denominational tenets may lead some to accept and others to reject, and that will be the case irrespective of how the study is conducted. So the distinction between teaching denominational formulae and teaching about denominational formulae may be unreal.

The fourth and perhaps the most important modification is that the agreed syllabuses must now 'reflect the fact that the religious traditions in Great Britain are in the main Christian, whilst taking into account the teaching and practices of the other principal religions represented in Great Britain'[5]. The content of syllabuses produced immediately after the 1944 Act was entirely Christian, usually consisting of Biblical study and Church history. The term 'religion' in those days was equated with 'Christianity'. Over the years, and especially since 1970, syllabuses have allocated an increasing amount of space to other faiths in response to the changing ethnological situation. Some have tried to justify this in their prefaces by redefining the aims of the subject.

The syllabus should be used to enlarge pupils' understanding of religion by studying world religions. (Birmingham, 1975)

Religious Education is most appropriately seen as an introduction to an individual's religious quest and some of its contemporary expressions in belief and practice rather than an induction into a particular religion. (Northamptonshire, 1980)

It is no part of the responsibility of a county school to promote any particular religious standpoint, neither can an exclusive Christian content do justice to the nature of the subject. (Hampshire, 1978)[6]

Some syllabuses, such as that of Cambridgeshire, have made statements to the effect that because Christianity is the religion that has most greatly influenced our culture it will be the one studied in greatest detail but the content of those syllabuses has not been significantly different from that of the others. The general trend has been to deal with Christianity as 'one of the world religions'.

The place of Christianity in the syllabuses

By asking that syllabuses be influenced by the fact that Christianity is the predominant tradition in the country, is the 1988 Act trying to reverse that process? Or is it drawing the attention of syllabus makers to an important factor that they have tended to forget in their enthusiasm to adapt to a changed climate of thought? The Act recognizes that religious traditions other than the Christian one must be appropriately represented, and many teachers, and other citizens, would agree that Christianity needs more time than some other faiths, because not only is it, as far as Britain is concerned, more extensive, diverse and complex, but also because, whatever may pertain in the future, it is the religion that is still most deeply and extensively conditioning the country's culture. Perhaps the brusque way in which this section of the Act is phrased (Any agreed syllabus *shall* reflect. etc.) gives the impression of desire to regulate the content of syllabuses in a way that was not intended, but the question of whether it is realistic or reactionary is likely to be the subject of hot debate.

Further there is the practical matter of what syllabuses must contain in order to be deemed acceptable. Will it suffice to make some such statement of intent as is found in the Cambridgeshire syllabus? Or must the amount of syllabus content which deals with Christianity be of greater length than that referring to other religions? If the latter, by how much should its length predominate? Such predominance would be difficult to establish if future syllabuses follow the recent practice of defining aims and objectives and saying almost nothing about content, leaving selection of that to the teachers who may choose what seems to them most likely to achieve the aims and reach the objectives. Or is it intended that the way the content is arranged and presented shall imply that a greater importance is to be attached to the Christian element in the culture? If the latter, this will provoke even hotter and more acrimonious debate and have considerable implications for the way the subject is taught and the choice of those to whom the teaching of it can be entrusted (see Chapter 8 on teachers' responsibilities).

Local arrangements for assessment and for syllabus construction and use
While core and foundation subjects are not only to have a nationally defined syllabus but also target and regular attainment tests for specified age groups, a similar provision is not made for religious education. However, the section of Schedule 5 of the 1944 Education Act, which permits a Syllabus Conference to recommend the inclusion in their proposals of attainment targets, programmes of study and assessment arrangements in locally determined form, is still operative and the DES Circular 3/89[7] records that 'the Secretary of State hopes that the possibility of doing so will be fully considered when an agreed syllabus is being reviewed'[8]. Recent syllabuses have usually provided targets, to some extent, in their lists of objectives, and they have been sufficiently similar to minimize the danger of different authorities setting widely differing targets.

Voting arrangements on Syllabus Conferences remain unchanged, as does the extent to which agreed syllabuses must be used in the educational system. The four panels of a Conference have each one vote when decisions are being made and they must all vote in agreement. This, in effect, gives each panel the right of veto and it may be thought that that gives a disproportionate power to the Church of England, which has a panel all to itself.

Agreed syllabuses have to be used in all maintained and controlled schools, but not in aided and special agreement schools. Provisions for the use of agreed syllabuses in any grant-maintained schools that may come into being are dealt with separately in Chapter 8. Parents who do not wish their children to be taught according to an agreed or any other syllabus may have them withdrawn. Should they wish them to be taught religious education of a kind not provided in the school, such pupils may be withdrawn to be taught elsewhere, either in a school that normally provides that kind of teaching, or according to special arrangements. Under certain circumstances special arrangements can be made for the requested teaching to be given in the school itself. In aided and special agreement schools, where an agreed syllabus is not normally used, parents may ask that their children be taught according to the agreed syllabus and arrangements have to be made for that to be done. These exceptional provisions have, of course, not to interfere drastically with the pupils' other education nor incur extra cost to the LEA. These facilities have been available ever since 1944, but they have not been frequently used. Whether the changed provisions of 1988 will cause more parents to use them remains to be seen.

If we enquire into the underlying reasons why it was decided to define the content of religious education by making syllabuses of this sort in this way it is possible to detect some confusion and certain ideas which need to be thought through further. The Government wants a school curriculum which will not only promote the development of pupils but which will also promote the spiritual, moral and cultural welfare of society. They seem to have been concerned that, because of the explosion of knowledge in this century and the coming into the country of groups from other cultures, there is danger of social and cultural disintegration in Britain, and certainly many would agree with them that our society is not as coherent as it was, neither so certain of its morality nor sharing the united vision that it once had. This has led to many problems of control and behaviour. In days gone by the vision that held society together was based on Christian ideals and expressed in Christian terms, and there is still a large residual element of Christianity. The government seems to be appealing to that residual element to recall some of the lost vision and coherence – hence the desire to have agreed syllabuses take into account the extent and influence of residual Christianity. But at the same time the government recognizes that there are strong pockets of other religions, sincerely held and practised, which are contributing to the development of the culture of the future, which cannot be ignored. So the government may be thought not to have had the courage of its convictions and legislated for an all out Christian syllabus, but passed on the problem to local authorities and required them to make syllabuses that both reflect the predominance of Christianity over the country as a whole and, at the same time, do justice to the religious mix in their own areas. In some localities this may be asking the near impossible.

It might have been possible to take the line that, just as in 1944 there was only one religion, Christianity, generally in evidence, but divided into denominations, so that syllabuses that defined what those denominations agreed could be taught accurately and without offence, so now, in a pluralist society of several respectable religions and some respectable secular philosophies, there is a need for an agreed inter-faith syllabus which could be nationally determined. The very fact of having to draw up such a syllabus would force people from diverse backgrounds and traditions to think out what national ethos would be coherent and acceptable to men and women of good will but of differing ways of expressing what they think to be of ultimate importance. There would be the risk that the religions which have arrived in Britain more recently, being geographically closely grouped and consequently more keenly aware of their religious identity, and feeling that they have to preserve that identity and get it accepted alongside the existing culture, would too greatly influence the syllabuses to the detriment of the Christian element. That this risk exists is shown by the tendency for religious education in some areas to consist of study of almost all religions except Christianity. But if Christianity genuinely has the predominant place in the culture that the Act implies, it ought to be able to hold its own. If the government is convinced that such is the case, a nationally determined inter-faith syllabus might have been worth considering.

References

1 *Education Reform Act 1988,* Sections 3 and 4.

2 Department of Education and Science (1989), *Circular 3/89; The Education Reform Act 1988: Religious Education and Collective Worship*, Section 20

3 *Education Reform Act 1988,* Section 7, 2a.

4 Ibid., Schedule 1, Section 1, 3.

5 Ibid., Section 8, 3.

6 Birmingham Agreed Syllabus, 1975, Introduction; Northamptonshire Agreed Syllabus, 1980, p.7; Hampshire Agreed Syllabus, 1978, Preface.

7 This is a document issued by the Department of Education and Science, addressed to local education authorities, heads and governing bodies of maintained schools, teacher training institutions, diocesan bodies, etc., to explain the Act and the manner in which it may be implemented.

8 Department of Education and Science (1989), *Circular 3/89; The Education Reform Act 1988: Religious Education and Collective Worship*, Section 20.

Chapter Five
Collective Worship in Schools
Education Reform Act 1988, Sections 6, 7 and 12
Edwin Cox

Ever since education began in Britain there has been worship in schools. It was taken for granted that regular religious observance was part of their daily life, but it was not until 1944 that it became a legal requirement. Both the 1944 Education Act and the 1988 Education Reform Act stipulate daily collective worship and both Acts mention it before they deal with teaching about religion in the classroom. That throws light on how the legislators thought of religious education. They saw it not just as the imparting of information about religion, but as giving some experience of the practice of religion. That was to be the ultimate outcome of the subject. Nor was it a matter of providing some religious experience to illustrate the teaching; rather that the teaching was to be the prelude to the worship – the giving of the necessary understanding that would make the worship meaningful.

School worship 1944-88
In 1944 it was not stated what form the worship was to take, but it was tacitly assumed that it would be Christian worship. In the House of Lords debate that preceded the passing of the Act it was said by Lord Clifford of Chudleigh: 'It is the intention of the Government ... that the corporate act of worship shall be an act of Christian worship.'[1] At that time there were in Britain few adherents of other religions and the only form of worship that most people could visualize was a Christian one. Not a great deal of thought was given to what form of worship is likely to be meaningful in schools. Consequently it was, for the most part, the sort of worship that is carried on in Church cut down to appropriate size. In the years immediately following 1944 pupils seem to have accepted this and

tolerated it as a normal aspect of school life. But many of them were not personally seriously involved in it and as time went by they became increasingly restive and critical of an activity which seemed to them to have little relevance to their lives. Added to this, the religious constitution of British society changed. Quite a number who had been previously nominally Christian, or had kept to themselves their private doubts about the acceptability of many aspects of Christian doctrine, found it possible to admit openly to being agnostic, or even atheist; whilst immigration brought to these shores not insignificant groups of people sincerely professing other faiths, Hindus, Muslims, Sikhs, etc. This made a Christian act of worship in schools even more problematic, and teachers expressed more freely their misgivings about it. Some schools continued in the old ways and still provided Christian acts of worship with optimistic disregard of the difficulties; others reduced worship to a minimum; whilst others experimented with multi-faith forms and assemblies that were moral and humanistic rather than religious.

Certain writers on education questioned the purpose of school worship. John Hull, in his book *School Worship: an obituary*[2] argued that the most that schools which were not attached to a religious denomination could hope to achieve was to bring pupils to 'the threshold of worship' rather than involve them in worship itself. The present writer, in his book *Problems and Possibilities for Religious Education*[3] found it necessary to include a note to the effect that it might ease the situation if the legal requirement of school worship were repealed, even if the provision for teaching about religions were maintained. Behind all these ideas and changes was the fact that the law was being increasingly difficult to keep, and was by no means universally heeded. Yet the 1988 Education Reform Act repeats the stipulation that all schools must provide a daily collective act of worship, and goes further in stating that it 'shall be wholly or mainly of a broadly Christian character'[4]. Obviously these revised provisions need to be studied in detail and their reasons, their implications and their feasibility discussed.

The 1988 provisions
The chief provisions for worship contained in the 1988 Act are comparatively simple, but the exceptions are complex. The law now makes it compulsory for all pupils, of all ages, in maintained schools to attend a daily act of collective worship, unless one of the exceptions applies to them. The collective worship, however, need no longer be at the beginning of the school day, nor is it necessary for all the school to be present at it at

one time – many schools are too large now for that to be possible, anyway. A single act of worship is still permitted but it is now also possible to organize separate acts of worship for age groups or 'school groups'. A school group is defined as any group in which the pupils are taught, or in which they take part in a school activity. This would seem to preclude groups specially convened for the worship sessions, based perhaps on common religious beliefs, so it would not be in the spirit of the Act to arrange for pupils of each religious belief to assemble for the sort of worship to which they are accustomed outside school. That approach to the problem of worship in a multicultural school seems barred.

As already noted, the worship is to be broadly Christian and reflect 'the broad traditions of Christian belief without being distinctive of any particular Christian denomination'[5]. There is a certain amount of flexibility and it is not necessary for the collective worship to be entirely Christian on every occasion. There can be other forms of worship provided that 'taking any school term as a whole' most of the worship is Christian. The term 'most' is indefinite and there is doubt as to how this injunction will be interpreted. What percentage will be regarded as qualifying to be described as 'most'? Already one has heard it said that the Act demands that 51 per cent of collective worship has to be Christian. Schools which provide collective worship in order to comply with the law, and not from conviction, may well try to sail as near to the wind as that. There is certainly going to be confusion and great diversity of practice until what is intended is clarified, or some tradition accepted and established. Furthermore the DES *Circular 3/89; The Education Reform Act 1988: Religious Education and Collective Worship* records that 'in the Secretary of State's view an act of worship which is "broadly Christian" need not contain only Christian material provided that, taken as a whole, it reflects the traditions of Christian belief'[6]. It is not easy to see what kind of non-Christian material the Secretary of State has in mind. Presumably it will not be anti-Christian, but will contain sentiments that are consonant with Christianity, but not in a form that has traditionally been used in Church services; it may be a form used in one of the other religions when that religion is expressing beliefs or sentiments that it has in common with Christianity; in either case there is some justification for thinking of it as being Christian material, even though shared with other belief systems. However unless the Secretary of State is taking a limited, narrowly traditional and stereotyped view of what qualifies as content for a Christian form of worship he may here be opening the way for the inclusion of a wide range of literature which, although not in explicitly religious language, is sensitive to the issues with which religion deals. The ability to use such material would give wider scope to those who have to plan collective worship in a multi-cultural situation and assist them in putting together acts of worship which have meaning for the pupils, while still keeping within the spirit of the legislation. Perhaps only experience will show how much of this non-Christian-specific material can be included without the worship being challenged as not broadly Christian, but this could be an important issue.

It is made clear who is responsible for seeing that the collective worship is available. In county schools it is the duty of the headteacher after consultation with the governing body; in voluntary schools it is the governing body after consultation with the headteacher. Presumably the difference is to allow the governing body of a voluntary school to ensure that the worship is in conformity with its trust deeds and ethos. Even if a headteacher does not wish to conduct the worship (and the 1944 provision that teachers in county schools cannot be required to take part in either religious teaching or religious worship still is operative) that head is responsible for seeing that the worship takes place and is conducted by a properly qualified and capable person, either one of the other teachers in the school or someone brought in from outside for that particular purpose.

So far we have been considering the overall application of the clauses in the 1988 Act relating to collective worship. We have now to consider the exceptions.

The worship in maintained schools is to take place on the school premises, but if governing bodies of aided schools, special agreement schools and the new grant-maintained schools (when they are established)

> are of the opinion that it is desirable that any collective act of worship in the school...should, on a special occasion, take place elsewhere than on the school premises, they may make such arrangements for that purpose as they think appropriate[7].

This will allow schools belonging to religious bodies to take their pupils into their places of worship for suitable religious observance on their festivals and holy days.

Parents have the right to ask that their children be excused attendance at school worship and that request has to be implemented. There is no provision in the Act for alternative forms of worship to be provided for those pupils (analogous to the possibility of providing alternative teaching for those withdrawn from religious education lessons) but DES Circular 3/39 makes the point that such alternative worship is not prohibited, and may take place provided denominational worship does not replace the statutory non-denominational collective worship and provided it does not entail additional cost to the school.[8]

There is a clause which allows parents to ask for extra forms of worship to be available for pupils in maintained boarding schools. If parents of such pupils request that they be allowed to attend worship on Sundays and other distinctively hallowed days, according to the religious tradition to which they belong, the governing body of the school must make reasonable arrangements for this to happen. It is even possible for arrangements to be made, if necessary, for such worship to take place on school premises, provided it does not involve extra expenditure by the governing body or the authority.

It is possible for a school to be permitted, in certain circumstances, to have worship which is not broadly Christian. The ages and aptitudes of the pupils, together with their family background (which presumably includes their family religion or lack of religion) have to be taken into account in deciding what form the school worship shall take. If a headteacher, after consultation with the governing body, is of the opinion that Christian worship, even of the broadest nature, is not appropriate for all or part of the pupils in the school, he or she may ask the Standing Advisory Council for Religious Education (see Chapter 7) for permission to provide some other form, either for the whole school or for groups within the school. It is suggested by DES Circular 3/89 that a head's decision to make such an application might be influenced by the extent of withdrawals from Christian collective worship.[9] The SACRE has the duty of deciding whether or not the proposed alternative form is allowable and must communicate its decision to the head in writing. That decision can be reviewed at any time at the headteacher's request and must be reviewed at the end of five years. At such a review the headteacher may make such representations as he or she, in consultation with the governing body, thinks fit. The Act suggests that the governing body may at this juncture see fit to seek the views of parents of registered pupils at the school. Possibly this is to assure the governing bodies that though they ought rightly to take account of parental wishes they need not consider the views of dogmatic partisan groups who for their own reasons wish to influence the school without having any direct connection with it.

It is to be noted that this machinery allows heads only to ask that the worship in their school be not broadly Christian. It does not permit them to ask that they be exempt from the main provision that all pupils must, unless parentally withdrawn, attend some sort of act of worship, and that their schools provide no worship at all. Nor does it allow them to ask that maintained schools should have worship of a Christian denominational character. Worship must still be provided which is not distinctive of any denomination, although the Act goes on to say 'this shall not be taken as preventing that worship from being distinctive of any particular faith'[10]. Presumably that means it may be broadly Jewish, broadly Islamic, broadly Hindu, etc., if those terms have any significance. Or did the authors of the Act not realize that there can be denominations in religions other than Christianity?

What are the problems?
To teachers who have struggled with the problems of providing in present-day schools some form of worship which is not an empty formality but has some meaning or significance for the collection of children of various faiths and doubts who are required to attend, the clauses in the 1988 Act may well seem blandly optimistic. The legislators appear to have assumed that because there has until recently always been in schools a form of worship that was principally Christian it is desirable that there always should be such, ignoring the fact that intellectual and sociological changes in the constitution of British society has made the provision of it more difficult and its justification less apparent. But it is questionable whether the present confusion about both its purpose and its practice can be removed simply by defining its content more closely and insisting on more consistent attendance at it. The whole matter of worship in schools needs to be more deeply thought out and there are a number of questions that need to be asked.

To begin with one would wish to ask why it is necessary to include worship in schools at all. It is not provided in most institutions which provide higher education, and even in those colleges in older universities which have religious origins, chapels and chaplains, it is not compulsory and frequently takes a minor part in college life. It is, of course, possible to argue that those institutions are dealing with more specialist education and can ignore those aspects of it that are not their primary concern, whereas at an earlier stage in the educational process all aspects of human experience must be included. Yet in the USA worship in non-Church schools is not only lacking, it is expressly forbidden. There education is considered to be adequate without religious observances. That settles nothing, of course, because the Americans may have an incomplete view of education, but it highlights the questions of what function worship plays in the formal educational process, and whether that function is a necessary part of the process.

Leaving aside those questions for the moment, there is the further matter of what insights the worship is intended to give to the pupils who take part. Is it to provide information, acquainting them with the ways in which those sections of the population who are religious variously behave, from time to time, when they are being expressly and corporately religious? If so, would that knowledge be more accurately acquired by taking them to observances in religious places of worship, where what goes on will have more genuine fervour than the average school assembly? Or does the fact that the material used in such observances will be too adult and belief-based to make sense to the young, mean that they need to be subjected to a special form that is more suited to their understanding? Or is worship part of the experiential function of education intended to enable the pupils actually to take part in worship and to experience the feelings that accompany it? To answer that question it is necessary to consider precisely what worship is, what are the necessary conditions for collective worship to have significance and whether it is possible to create those conditions in the schools of a society that includes both a religious pluralism and considerable agnostic and secular elements.

Pre-requisites of worship
Worship is too complicated an activity for it to be defined by a simple formula. A crude definition might be that worship is talking to a God in order to pay homage, to discover what that God demands in human action, and expressing willingness and seeking resolution to obey those demands. That, however, raises further questions of what impels people to wish to talk to a God and whether there is any virtue in doing the talking communally or collectively rather than individually. If we are to investigate the role of worship in education we shall need to look at these deeper questions and examine more precisely what worship is, why it is undertaken and what it is expected to achieve.

The desire to worship seems to spring from a sense of something beyond oneself and the created world, something transcendent, which demands some kind of recognition and response. Not everyone reacts in the same way to that sense of the transcendent and much depends on the beliefs and assumptions that a person brings to it. Yet it is possible to divide the experiences of the transcendent, which underlie worship, into two types.

1. A generalized feeling of awe, a feeling that one has come into contact with a mystery that evokes wonder, a sense of eternity, a sense of truth, a sense of abasement etc., but which is not centred on a specific or definable object. Researchers into religious experience ranging from William James[11] and E. D. Starbuck[12] at the beginning of the century to Edward Robinson[13] and David

Hay[14] at the present time, say that feelings of this sort come to most people at some time. Whether the experience is interpreted in religious or in secular terms depends on the prior beliefs of those having the experience. Many respond in ways that cannot strictly be called religious, and do not think it necessary to link up with others who have had similar experiences and react in a communal way.

2. A feeling that the experience has brought one into contact with the origin and secret of the universe. This interpretation is probably confined to those who have already acquired a belief in a God and some conception of the nature of that God, and their response is likely to be more specific, leading to meditation, praise, adoration, self-abasement, confession and supplication. Furthermore viewed this way the experience is more likely to lead to joining with others who have a similar view of God in order to worship together and thereby achieve the intensity that attends genuine communal worship. It is this second response that religious bodies usually have in mind when they talk of worship, and they are inclined to regard the generalized response of 1. above as being 'the threshold of worship' rather than worship itself.

We are left with the question of which of these two types of response to a sense of the transcendent is envisaged by the Education Reform Act? Presumably both, since the second is dependent on the first and is a more closely defined form of it. Only the hardened materialist would object to pupils being exposed to feelings of wonder and awe, since they are part of common human experience, and are occasioned by subjects in school other than religious education, – music, literature, the relationships of mathematics, the interaction of matter dealt with in the sciences, may all lead to such apprehensions. However, the fact that the Act calls for collective worship makes it clear that responses of the second, and more specifically belief – based sort, are intended. That makes it necessary to enquire into the conditions under which that response is possible.

Communal worship can take place only if it is underpinned by a common belief system. Those who take part in it will find it fully satisfying only if they have a shared belief in a God, some agreement as to what that God is like and what demands that deity makes upon them. There must be the further beliefs that God communicates to humans through transcendental and prayer experiences, and that humans can, for their part, communicate with God through the worship, and that worshipping together is especially efficacious. To require school children to worship together assumes that they have those beliefs and to stipulate that it shall be mainly Christian assumes that the majority of them have beliefs that they envisage in Christian terms. Before going on to examine whether this is so, it may be worth noting that the Act speaks of 'collective' rather than of 'corporate' or 'communal' worship. That could mean that what is intended is that pupils should daily assemble for worship but not necessarily all worship in the same way, each one finding an appropriate 'depth' or 'transcendental' experience in reacting to the type of religious observance provided. That probably happens anyway, but the phrasing of the Act suggests that something less individualistic is intended.

Pupils' reaction to collective worship
If belief in a God and agreement as to the nature of that God is a pre-requisite of collective worship, we have next to consider whether those conditions are present in the average school at the present time. The 1944 Act took it for granted that Britain was a homogeneous Christian believing society and that there would be no problem about worship in schools. The new Act seems to take it for granted that the situation has not greatly changed, but it is difficult to think that this is the case. We now have a pluralist society in which there is a great number of religious people, but also an appreciable number who would describe themselves as agnostic and atheist. There are not a few to whom any form of religion is totally unimportant. These views are found among pupils in schools, certainly in the upper forms. The Martin and Pluck research[15] carried out among adolescents and young adults in east London in the late 1970s showed that most of them had little idea of religious belief and regarded religion as something they had now grown out of, something irrelevant to their lives, something suitable only for young children and the superstitious. More-over the religious section of the population is more diverse than it used to be, including not only Christians but practising Muslims, Jews, Hindus, Sikhs, etc. The Act, in its assumption that all pupils will be able to respond to a broadly Christian form of worship, does not seem to have taken this pluralism completely seriously. It does make allowance for those of other faiths but makes no concession to those of no faith at all.

However, this does not invalidate what it is trying to do. There is a case for making available to children the possibility of transcendental experi-ence and introducing them to the sort of religious response to life that many still find important and indulge in regularly. Not to do so would mean that their education was failing in its duty to help them understand life in its fullness and to develop in themselves all the capacities for involvement in, and enjoyment of life. Not all children will respond negatively to the possibility of worship. Some will, but others may find in it a significance which enriches their life and which will continue into adulthood. The fact that some cannot find meaning in it is no argument for denying it to those who can. Furthermore, in the present state of social evolution in Britain, although there are in certain places groups professing allegiance to other world faiths who must be recognized and catered for, in wide areas Christianity remains the major religion practised. The Christian form of worship consequently is the one that will seem normal to the majority and the one to which they most easily respond and relate. At the same time it must be remembered that in many schools there will be pupils whose beliefs will not allow them to respond fully to Christian forms of worship, whose consciences must be respected, and who must be encouraged not to allow their non-participation to inhibit the full participation of those who can respond.

For all the misgivings expressed above, the legal provisions for school worship may be concerned with something that is essential as part of education; questions remain, however, about whether those provisions are the right ones for the concerns to be realised. The Act does not seem to make much allowance for the problems of providing mainly Christian worship in multicultural schools. Is it conceiving of school worship in too narrow a way, setting to it bounds that are too rigid for the desired outcome to emerge?

Much will depend on how the words 'wholly or mainly of a broadly Christian character' are interpreted by heads, by the inspectorate and by the SACREs. This phrase, while recognizing the predominant place that Christianity still occupies among the religions practised in Britain, does permit schools to have non-Christian forms of collective worship from time to time, thereby not only catering for those who belong to other religions but also making it possible for children to learn and appreciate something of forms of worship they have not previously encountered, which will in turn help them to understand those who regularly use those forms. It is not clear whether non-theistic forms of worship, which think seriously about life and its purpose, and the more generalized experiences of the transcendent mentioned above (which do not necessarily involve reference to personal spiritual beings), are permitted; but they are not explicitly forbidden and some may think them appropriate for pupils who wish to think about life seriously but do not find any religion helpful. There may be heads who, because of the depth and exclusiveness of their own religious convictions, will interpret the Act as calling for total and exclusive Christian content and hope that the worship will lead to

Christian evangelism, and paranoiac secularists will doubtless insist that this will be general. But the possibility of a certain degree of non-Christian worship, and the provision that heads may ask SACREs for permission to be exempt from this clause of the Act, would seem to indicate that heads have considerable freedom in designing the type of worship that will be most sensible and sincere in their particular school. The provisions may not be quite as restrictive as they appear on the surface to be.

There are some practical problems about school worship that still have to be considered. Collective worship takes on depth in proportion to the number present who are sincerely taking part. Complaints have been made in the past about its formality and perfunctoriness because of pupils' inability to begin to join in. That may still be the case. It is all very well for politicians to compel pupils to attend but they cannot command how they think while they are present. This is a weakness in the philosophy behind the Act, which will be minimized only if those who plan the worship are imaginative and subtle in the choice of stimulating material – if such can be found. In that connection the requirement to provide worship daily is likely to be a burden. It is an exacting task to find varied and lively material day after day, and there will be some excuse if there is a certain amount of repetition and lack of inspiration. The National Association of Head-teachers pointed out in 1985 in their pamphlet *Religious Education in Schools*[16] that daily worship is 'a stricter requirement than Christian Churches lay upon their committed adult believers'. In most religions daily collective worship is asked only of priests and monastic orders. One wonders if to collect in schools so frequently is fully necessary and whether it may not be counter-productive.[17]

The imprecision of the term 'broadly Christian' is discussed in Chapter 6, but there is likely to be uncertainty about what a worship that 'reflects the broad traditions of Christian belief without being distinctive of any particular Christian denomination' will be like. Does it mean that only those forms of expression that are used by all Christian denominations (such as the Lord's Prayer and certain common hymns) can be used? Or does it mean that any material can be included, provided Christians of all sorts do not disapprove of it but feel they can relate to it? It could be argued that denominational forms of worship have arisen because they seem to a section of Christians sincerely to express a tradition of Christian belief and that worship taken out of its denominational clothing will have only remote connection with traditional Christianity, and that, if this is so, the Act is self-contradictory. Possibly no more is intended than that any Christian materials can be used provided they are not arranged in the order in which they would be found in a denominational church.

What will it achieve?

Behind these practical matters there lies the basic question of what school worship is intended to achieve. Why have it at all? In a religious setting corporate worship is an activity in which a group, with shared beliefs, respond to the God in whom they believe, and contemplate the implications of their beliefs; its aim is to clarify, intensify and express those beliefs. But a school is not a church nor a religious community; so what effect is the worship intended to have on the worshippers? It is possible that the government sees it as part of an endeavour to bring some kind of coherence and shared vision to a society which has become disunited as a result of a massive increase in knowledge and its application in technology, an uncritical and often intolerant liberalism with its attendant permissiveness, and the rapid mixing of diverse cultures as the result of rapid travel and migration. These factors have led to a good deal of unrest and many social problems. The present government may feel that it has to do something to deal with those problems and help to restore some agreed vision of the good and the just (see Chapter 10). They may feel that such a vision can arise only if people have a philosophy which goes beyond the mundane, and in that they may have the support of more of the population than a study of television advertising and the stories selected for publication in the tabloid press would suggest. Because British culture still retains strong elements of its Christian background, the provision that the young shall at least have the opportunity of coming into contact with Christian practices and being influenced by them, if those practices are judged by the young to be worthy of respect, is not unreasonable. Whether being exposed to school worship which does not give adequate recognition to other forms of worship now practised in Britain, or take account of pupils to whom all forms of worship are strange, will greatly assist pupils to come to a shared vision of the good and the just could be questioned.

If the purpose of legislating for daily and mainly Christian worship in schools is to do something, however indirect, to bring coherence of vision to succeeding generations, then to confine it to those forms which have pertained up to now is not the way to set about it. Those forms have been used in the past and become progressively ineffective, and the language in which worship is expressed is so alien as to be meaningless to most children. Much thought will have to be given to what forms of worship are appropriate in the school situation, what will evoke in pupils a sense of the transcendent and cause them to wonder and think – and that may be very different from worship in a believing situation. The Act requires that school worship take into account the circumstances, the family backgrounds and the ages and aptitudes of the pupils. It must also take into account the way their attitudes to religion condition their reaction to the worship. If the new provisions are to lead to anything more than a continuation of the unsatisfactory observances that have often, in recent decades, passed for school worship, a good deal of hard thinking will have to be done. It is not going to be as easy as the Act seems to imply.

References

1 *Parliamentary Debates (Hansard),* 4th Series, 132,366.

2 Hull, J. (1974), *School Worship: an Obituary.* London: SCM Press.

3 Cox, E. (1983), *Problems and Possibilities for Religious Education.* London: Hodder and Stoughton.

4 *Education Reform Act 1988,* Section 7,1.

5 Ibid., Section 7,2.

6 Department of Education and Science (1989), *Circular 3/89; The Education Reform Act 1988: Religious Education and Collective Worship*, Section 34.

7 *Education Reform Act 1988,* Section 6,5.

8 Department of Education and Science (1989), *Circular 3/89; Education Reform Act 1988: Religious Education and Collective Worship* Section 42.

9 Ibid., Section 36.

10 *Education Reform Act 1988,* Section 7,6,b.

11 James, W. (1902), *The Varieties of Religious Experience.* New York: Longman.

12 Starbuck, E. D. (1899), *The Psychology of Religion.* New York: Walter Scott.

13 Robinson, E. (1983), *The Original Vision.* New York: Seabury Press.

14 Hay, D. (1987), *Exploring Inner Space.* London: Mowbrays Press.

15 Martin, B. and Pluck, R. (1977), *Young People's Beliefs.* London: Church of England Board of Education.

16 National Association of Head Teachers (1985), *Religious Education in Schools.*

17 Recognising the difficulty of what schools were being asked to do, leaders of the Christian churches urged that the requirements for daily collective worship be modified, but the Secretary of State did not see fit to respond to their advice.

Chapter Six
Broad Traditional Christianity
Education Reform Act 1988, Sections 7, 1 and 8, 3
Edwin Cox

As we have seen, the 1944 Education Act legislated for religious education, comprising worship and religious instruction, but stopped short of stating what religion was intended. It was generally assumed that Christianity was meant and Christianity was the religion that formed the content of subsequent practice and agreed syllabuses. Maybe the 1944 legislators ought to have had the courage of their convictions and stated that Christian religious education was what they had in mind, but their failure to do so has allowed some flexibility in the more recent teaching and permitted the inclusion of material concerning the other religions now found in Britain.

The new 1988 Act goes some way towards specifying Christianity, but, because it has been obliged to take some account of the religious and social changes that have occurred in the intervening years, it does so in an indirect and tentative way. The teaching is to reflect the mainly Christian nature of British religious traditions and the majority of the worship is to be broadly Christian. One cannot help but wonder what these terms precisely mean and what kind of teaching and worship would be thought to meet them.

Reflecting Christian religious traditions
The teaching is not to be exclusively Christian; it must take into account the other principal religious teaching and practices, while 'reflecting' the mainly Christian religious traditions of the country. Teachers will doubt-less ask what this means and what content and method of teaching is involved.

There are several possible ways of interpreting this clause (Section 8.3) of the Act. It could mean that children are to be taught that up to the present, Christianity has been the chief religious influence in the culture and to be given some knowledge of the extent and nature of that influence. This would involve discussion of its effect on literature, art, the legal and ethical system, etc., which would be welcomed by some teachers of other subjects, who complain that their work is handicapped by pupils' ignorance of the Christian ideas that are assumed in older literature and art. Such an approach would do justice to the historical influence of Christianity, and the taking account of other principal religions would provide for the new pluralistic culture that has superseded it. Christianity would be included in those principal religions and taught as one of the world faiths. In other words the Act is recognizing what has become accepted practice and no change is required. This interpretation, however, seems at odds with the general tenor of the Act, which does not say that the past influences on British culture have been mainly Christian, but that the *religious traditions* in Great Britain *are* mainly Christian. Teaching more directly about present Christian influences seems intended.

What kind of teaching would 'reflect' that influence? The word 'reflect' is difficult, suggesting that the teaching is not to be direct but to convey the desired impression obliquely, but that is perhaps an example of the difficulty of Parliamentary drafting and it would be pedantic to make too much of it. The general intention seems to be that religious education has to try and convince pupils that Christianity is still a faith to be respected, which has the greatest following in the country and is still making an effective and beneficent contribution to the ethos and development of the culture. How far that is in fact the case is debatable, but it is a view that would probably command a wide, if uninformed, support from the population generally.

Nevertheless, the phrasing of this clause of the Act has given some offence and caused concern among the religious bodies that are not Christian. That schools are to teach about them as well is relegated, in Section 8,3 of the Act, to a subordinate clause ('whilst taking account..', etc.) and that gives them the impression that they have not been considered as seriously as they might have been. They would have liked some positive statement that it will be possible for their children to be taught about their own faith. The clause may have been so phrased because of their relatively small number, rather than out of lack of respect for them, but it is certainly insensitive, and some alleviation of it in the form of reassurance from the DES may be advisable.

There remains the question of whether it is intended that the reflecting shall be achieved by selection of content or by method of teaching. Since the relevant clause (Section 8) is described as 'Religious education required in the basic curriculum' it may be intended to cover content only. In that case, what proportion of the syllabus must be allotted to it? Will it suffice, as some recent agreed syllabuses have done, to state that Christianity is to be studied in greatest detail, or will it require that Christianity shall have a major space in the description of content to be studied? If the latter, many recent syllabuses will need revision, since they are deliberately not lists of content. And will the 1975 Birmingham syllabus, which says that Christianity is to be studied by all secondary school pupils, but not necessarily as a major study, become illegal? Another view might be that it is not the extent of the Christian content of the syllabus that matters but the type of content. If less time were allocated to Christian doctrine and practice, and to Bible study, and more to the geographical spread of Christianity in the British Isles and its effect on culture and morals, pupils might get clearer insight into its place in the culture, but that would take the subject from religious studies to sociology, and still fail to give pupils any appreciation of what Christianity is essentially about and why it has such a following and influence.

Even greater problems are encountered if we consider whether achieving the objectives of this part of the Act necessitates a particular teaching method. Since this section of the Act is specifically relating to agreed syllabuses one would not have supposed that method was affected, did not a later clause (Section 11,2) permit Standing Advisory Councils to include method of teaching in their reviews of how the agreed syllabuses are used. If it really is intended that teaching methods be employed that stress the predominance of the Christian religious tradition, the question arises of what methods will achieve that end without involving a high degree of partiality. Will such methods not come dangerously near to indoctrination and will teachers who are not militantly Christian be prepared to employ them? The Act may not intend this, but its imprecision at this point lays it open to misinterpretation by pressure groups who wish to use education to advance their own causes.

Probably the references in the Act to Christianity being the main religious tradition were meant to do no more than redress the imbalance that has arisen in places since schools began to teach about non-Christian religions. There has been a temptation for teachers to spend more time on other religions than Christianity, partly because of their novelty value, and partly because restless adolescents, who have reacted against aspects of Christian doctrine and mythology, can be more easily persuaded to give attention to other faiths, in the hope that they may find less in them to conflict with their rationalist and 'scientific' assumptions. The result is sometimes that Christianity has come to have less than its appropriate share of the teaching in certain schools. If the Act is calling attention to this and asking for a realistic balance in future, then it would be difficult fairly to quibble about it. This section of the Act is, however, somewhat obscure and is likely to cause problems both of interpretation and implementation. It has been discussed here, not with the hope of defining it (that is for the Government and the DES, not for commentators), or of solving the problems, but to draw attention to the difficulties and to the need of further thought in this area.

Broad Christianity

That school worship is to be of a broadly Christian character is looking back to the days when Christian denominations were mutually antagonistic and jealously guarded their distinctive beliefs and practices. Then county schools had carefully to confine themselves to material common to all denominations. If that is what is required, now the range of material is much greater, and provided school worship does not include references to doctrines and ceremonies that are peculiarly denominational and likely to evoke a residual emotional opposition in some quarters (such as, for instance, the hagiolatry of the Roman Catholic Church, the transubstantial aspects of the Mass, the Calvinist teaching of election or the strict Baptist attitude to baptism) then there should be no difficulty in compiling varied and legal forms of worship. Whether those forms will evoke ready response from the pupils is another matter and discussed in Chapter 5.

There is a still wider meaning that can be attached to the term 'broadly Christian'. The term 'broad church' used to be applied to certain sections of the Church of England that found little meaning in the more arcane aspects of doctrine and the minutiae of liturgical worship, but saw Christianity as a civilizing and moral outlook, a code of decency and good neighbourliness. Being Christian meant generally following that code and occasionally recognizing its connection with ecclesiastical theology by a visit to church. Such an outlook is still widely held, perhaps more especially in the rural middle classes, from which many supporters of the present government come, and has been referred to as a folk faith. It recognizes the existence of a guiding providence, which is approached in prayers in times of necessity, accepts the wisdom and moral teaching of Jesus but is not concerned with Christological doctrines, approves of the Ten Commandments (even though breaking the fourth and seventh have long since ceased to be regarded as sinful and breaking the tenth is looked on as a laudable spur to success), and, if asked what Christianity is, quotes the Golden Rule. Its religiosity often finds expression in hymnody outside church worship, in listening to televized hymn singing, in joining in 'Jerusalem' at the last night of Promenade Concerts, and in 'Abide with Me' at football matches. It responds to short religious services at Remembrance Day ceremonies and keeps some connection with the organized church for baptisms and funerals. It is not impossible that this folk faith is stronger in the older part of the population, for whom the hymns have nostalgic memories of church-going youth, and that the younger generations feel it less.

One is not decrying this folk faith, merely querying whether this is what is meant in the Act by 'broadly Christian'. If so, what will the worship that properly results from it be like? It will not be doctrinal or markedly liturgical. What assumptions will it presuppose in those who join in it and those who lead it? Will those who are not Christian find it easier to participate than they would if it were more markedly theological? Will this mixture of partly Christian and partly humanist ideals win a response from, and have some lasting effect on, those who daily attend school worship, even though it may not satisfy those of a deeply religious or philosophical turn of mind? Here again the Act seems not to have succeeded in its attempt to define what in future is to happen in schools, but to have left all the problems that beset school worship in the past, and added to them the new one of how to be broadly Christian.

Chapter Seven
Standing Advisory Councils on Religious Education
Education Reform Act 1988, Sections 11 – 13
Edwin Cox

It is one thing to pass an Act of Parliament but it is another to ensure that it is effective. In some instances Parliament relies widely on the good will and the law-abiding instinct of citizens to see that its injunctions are obeyed, though there are usually penalties prescribed for those who step out of line. In other, more serious, instances, a monitoring system is set up, such as the police or the tax fraud investigation machinery, backed by the courts and the penal system to enforce law-keeping.

On the whole, laws relating to education fall into the first category. Teachers and school governors are credited with being respectable citizens and entrusted with implementing the law. The Inspectorate, both national and local, have provided encouragement to carry out the positive injunctions of educational legislation, but there have been few cases of punitive action being taken when the law has been broken. With the wide nature of the school system, where education is carried on a little removed from direct public scrutiny, it is difficult to see how it could be otherwise. Certainly it is difficult to envisage in Britain the schools being subject to constant detailed surveyance by the constabulary, or some similar body, to enforce the Education Acts in every particular.

The history of Standing Advisory Councils
Nevertheless, teachers have not always strictly followed their law-abiding instincts; the religious provisions of the 1944 Act have been sometimes cavalierly observed, and on occasions totally disregarded. If the purpose of the 1988 Act is to reiterate those provisions, and to see that they are more strictly observed, there arises the question of how to ensure effective

compliance with them. The alarm that some educators have expressed about them suggests that their law-abiding instincts may be under some pressure. It is possible that the Inspectorate will be more insistent on religious education complying with the law. But it would appear that the government is placing some reliance on Standing Advisory Councils on Religious Education to take a leading role in monitoring how religion is dealt with in schools.

These councils, usually referred to as SACREs, are not new. The 1944 Education Act permitted local education authorities to set one up if they so wished; it did not specify the constitution of the Councils, and it was left to the decision of the local authorities who would be invited to serve on them[1]. Some authorities took advantage of this permission and convened a SACRE and others did not. Quite what these SACREs achieved it is difficult to assess. Doubtless many of them took an informed interest in religious education in their neighbourhood and offered wise and helpful advice. Others have sometimes been slow to recognize the value of the curriculum development that teachers were advocating as desirable. This, of course, was salutary when it prevented over-enthusiastic and irresponsible experimentation, but occasionally it stood in the way of the subject responding sensitively to cultural, intellectual and theological change. Religious education in those authorities that did not choose to convene SACREs does not seem to have been greatly deprived, and consequently one can only wonder whether SACREs had sufficient power to be significantly influential.

Their new constitution

The 1988 Act, however, makes it compulsory for SACREs to be constituted by all authorities and specifies how they are to be constituted. They are to have the same four panels as the Agreed Syllabus Conferences (representatives of the Church of England, the local authority, teachers' associations and 'such Christian and other religious denominations as, in the opinion of the authority, will appropriately reflect the principle religious traditions in the area'[2]). This may compound the confusion that sometimes exists about the difference between the SACREs and the Agreed Syllabus Conferences. The same persons frequently serve on both but technically they are distinct bodies. A SACRE is a Standing Council, that is one in permanent existence; a Syllabus Conference is constituted only when a syllabus needs to be made or revised and is disbanded when its task has been completed. In each body voting is by panels, each panel having one vote, and in Syllabus Conferences the voting has to be unanimous for a decision to be made; the Act does not appear to require such unanimity in SACREs. This may account for the fact that when a Syllabus Conference fails to achieve total agreement it can appeal to the Secretary of State to adjudicate; SACREs have not been given such a right of appeal.

The defining of the constitution of a SACRE is an important change. Though it gives the Church of England a strong presence, religions other than Christianity must have representatives provided they are established in the area. The stipulation that they must have a local presence could have an unfortunate side-effect because it means that in those parts of the country where there are no strong bodies of other faiths the spectrum of religions will not be represented on the local SACRE, even though it may be thought desirable for the schools to teach something about world religions in order to fit the pupils for life in a multicultural world. The implication is that the authors of the Act saw religious education as dealing only with the faiths found in the vicinity of the school.

Two other types of person may be members of SACREs. There is power to co- opt, and in areas where there emerges one of the 'grant-maintained schools' that the Act permits, and that school teaches religious education in accordance with the LEA's Agreed Syllabus, the governing body of that school may appoint someone to represent it on SACRE. Where there is more than one grant-maintained school then their governing bodies have the right jointly to appoint a person to represent all of them[3]. Since voting in SACREs is by panels and representatives of grant-maintained schools do not belong to any panel, one has to assume that they will be able to contribute to discussion but have no voting power.

Appointments to serve on SACREs are made by the LEA, who must 'take all reasonable steps' to ensure that appointees are representative of the denominations and associations for whom they speak, and if at a later date a member ceases to be so representative of a denomination, association or authority he or she can be removed from the Council. Those who actually teach religious education still have no direct right to seats on SACREs, but the DES Circular 3/89; says that the Secretary of State 'believes that there would be advantage in ensuring that members representing associations of teachers include teachers of religious educa- tion'[4]. Teachers of religious education will doubtless be grateful for that small recognition of their contribution to the development of their subject. Nor does the Act prescribe how SACREs are to be chaired and funded, which matters are, one must assume, left to decision by the LEA. Circular 3/89, however, states that 'the Secretary of State' expects each LEA to provide a clerk for the Council and sufficient funds for it to perform its functions'[5].

Their function

The chief function of a SACRE is to 'advise the authority upon matters connected with religious worship in county schools and the religious education to be given in accordance with an agreed syllabus'[6]. In particular it is to concern itself with methods of teaching, choice of materials and the provision of training of teachers. In general it will deal with matters that are referred to it by the LEA, but it is not required to confine itself to those matters. The Act specifically states that it may deal with other matters that it 'may see fit'. Two specific duties, however, are laid upon SACREs. Firstly, they may at any time require a review of the agreed syllabus being used by the schools of the authority they serve and the authority must respond and set up a Syllabus Conference, which will at least reconsider the existing syllabus. Secondly, they have to consider requests from headteachers that the collective worship in their particular schools should not be Christian, and decide whether or not it is appropriate that some other form of collective worship be provided in those schools.

SACREs must give a yearly account of their proceedings in the form of an annual report, and according to the Circular 3/89, 'the Secretary of State believes that LEAs should arrange for copies of annual reports to be distributed to schools, and to the National Curriculum Council and local teacher training institutions'[7]. Such reports must give an account of:

1. Matters on which the SACRE has advised the LEA.
2. The nature of the advice that has been given.
3. Where it has offered advice for which the LEA has not asked, the reasons why it has thought fit to do so.

It looks as if the government regards SACREs as the watchdogs who are to see that the religious clauses of the Act are implemented. They are to watch what happens in the classroom and make sure that the content of religious education conforms with the law, that the methods used are effective and that the teachers have been trained in both the content and the methods. Furthermore they are to keep a watch on the LEA to see that it is supportive, that it provides as far as possible adequate resources and teaching staff, and that its syllabus is up to date and conforms with legal specifications. This raises the question of whether they are so constituted and have the powers effectively to perform those functions.

In the first place they will need to know what is actually happening in schools and have an insight into the problems of teaching about religion in a multicultural and partly secular age. They will need to appreciate how children think at the various stages of their growth and to sympathize with teachers' assessments of what is possible. Much will depend, therefore, on the personnel who are appointed to the councils. In the past SACREs have sometimes included members who, although influential and prestigious in the denominations and associations they represented, had insufficient connection with teaching to make informed contributions to educational discussions. It is to be hoped that the new SACREs will contain people who not only speak for their associations and for public opinion generally, but can also contribute detailed knowledge of classroom situations and procedures. The wish of the Secretary of State that there will be a number who are actually teaching the subject is important. Even so there are bound to be occasions when a SACRE will need further information about how the subject is being handled in schools if it is to offer wise advice to the LEA. Whether or not members of councils will think it necessary themselves to visit schools to seek that knowledge (or always be welcomed if they do so) remains to be seen, but certainly there will be needed some machinery whereby a SACRE can gather information about the content, the methods, the resources of the subject, as well as the racial constitution of schools, the attitudes and inclinations of teachers, and the problems that arise in connection with worship and religious teaching in the schools over which they are charged to keep watch.

In the second place there is the matter of what powers are available to a SACRE to see that its advice is taken seriously. The only direct power given it by the Act is the ability to require the LEA to set up a Syllabus Conference to consider (though not necessarily revise) the syllabus in use. Otherwise all that it can do is advise and hope that its advice will be acted upon. The final decision lies with the LEA, which, one presumes, will usually trust its SACRE and take heed, but there is no provision for what is to be done if the LEA proves unheedful or recalcitrant. SACREs may, however, have an indirect influence through their annual reports, especially if these are circulated round the schools and elsewhere. If such reports help create public opinion in favour of what SACREs advise, LEAs will be under pressure to respond and to take suitable action. There is nothing in the Act which permits a SACRE to appeal to a higher authority, such as the DES or the Secretary of State, if it feels it is unable adequately to discharge its function. It is, in this respect a watchdog with only one tooth. The Act is ultimately relying, as previously, on the goodwill and law-abiding instincts of the local authority and the schools to ensure that its clauses are respected and obeyed. Which, should it succeed, is perhaps as well in a civilized and democratic society.

References

1   *Education Act 1944,* Section 29, 2 and 3.

2   *Education Reform Act 1988,* Section 11, 4a.

3   Ibid., Section 11, 3b.

4   Department of Education and Science (1989), *Circular 3/89; The Education Reform Act 1988: Religious Education and Collective Worship*, Section 17.

5   Ibid., Section 18.

6   *Education Reform Act 1988,* Section 11, 1a.

7   Department of Education and Science (1989), *Circular 3/89; The Education Reform Act 1988: Religious Education and Collective Worship*, Section 14.

Chapter Eight
Teachers, Sixth Forms and Grant-maintained Schools
Edwin Cox

Teachers

The assumptions of the 1944 Act about what qualification teachers would need in order to teach religious education competently in the various types of schools have been tacitly continued in 1988. Those who deal with the subject in county schools must be qualified to teach according to the adopted agreed syllabus; teachers in aided schools must be able to teach in accord with trust deeds or the practice of the schools; in controlled schools the teachers must generally be competent to give agreed syllabus instruction, but there may be a number of teachers who are fit to teach according to the religious traditions of the school before it became controlled. These latter are called 'reserved' teachers and may not exceed in number one-fifth of the total staff.[1]

Saving provisions for teachers

Section 30 of the 1944 Education Act allows teachers to opt not to give religious instruction or to attend school worship. The 1988 Education Reform Act does not repeat that section, nor does it emend or repeal it, so that the earlier provision still applies. By it no teacher 'shall be disqualified by reason of his religious opinions, or of his attending or omitting to attend religious worship'[2] (there being less sensitivity in those days than there is now about using masculine pronouns and possessive adjectives to refer to all teachers). Furthermore no teacher could be required to give religious instruction, or receive less remuneration, or be disadvantaged for promotion or in any other way by reason of not doing so. This did not apply to teachers in aided or special agreement schools or to reserved teachers in controlled schools, but the Act was careful to stipulate that such teachers could not be paid less or otherwise disadvantaged because they gave religious teaching. One might assume that this was included to prevent the religious bodies taking advantage of keenness on the part of believers to give religious instruction.

That teachers can elect not to teach religious education and claim legal justification for that choice implies that the subject itself is peculiar, different in some way from other subjects. There can be an emotional aversion to it which can be made the grounds for conscientious objection in a way that does not apply to other school activities. One can understand teachers asking not to teach music because of tone deafness, or art because of colour-blindness, or mathematics and geography because of lack of knowledge of those disciplines, but that would be a matter of competence not of conscience. One may not be attracted to a subject but as long as one regards it as a fit topic for education one can hardly refuse to have anything to do with it. What is there, then, about religious education that makes it appropriate for conscientious avoidance? Is there a hidden assumption behind the legal provision for opting out that it is necessary to be religious in some way in order to teach it and that lack of a faith is comparable to tone deafness in the case of music and colour-blindness in the case of art? Or is the assumption that some teachers may feel so averse to its educational desirability that they must be allowed to protest about its presence by means of boycott? If that is so, the case for having religious education in all schools has not been fully established. Or are these safeguards of teachers' consciences merely a reflection of the ambivalence and worried suspicion that attends thinking about religion in a largely secular culture so that every exception has to be made whenever its presence or its absence have to be taken into account? It is not the purpose here to answer those questions, but merely to point out that the conscience clauses for teachers make religious education conspicuously different from other subjects and suggest that its rationale as an ingredient of education has not been fully thought out. If the aims of religious education, and the content with which it deals, had been totally accepted so that it was seen by all as a needed part of schooling, and as capable of being taught by defensible educational methods, then disinclination on the part of teachers to undertake it could have been dealt with in schools as are other reasonable aversions, and the conscience clauses (both for teachers and parents) in the Act would have been unnecessary.

Teacher supply and training
Not entirely unconnected with the foregoing is the type of training that is needed for those who are going to teach religious education under the new Act. What knowledge and insights do individuals have to acquire in order

that their teaching will 'reflect the fact that religious traditions in Great Britain are in the main Christian whilst taking account of the teaching and practices of the other principal religions represented in Great Britain'[3]? That could mean that in each school there has to be a preponderance of religious education teachers who have studied mainly Christianity (and are sufficiently versed in social history to appreciate the influence of Christianity on British institutions and traditions), with a number of others who can cope with the teaching and practice of the other religions. But few schools will have large enough religious education staffs for that to be viable. If the Act is to be fully implemented teachers will need to have specialist knowledge about Christianity and its influence on British culture and more than a working knowledge about other religions. Moreover if they are to relate to pupils who are influenced by secular belief systems they will need to know about those as well. The knowledge will have to be more than superficial if the teaching is going to do more than skim surfaces and if teachers are to be able confidently to deal with questions that enquiring pupils will ask. Therefore, unless the number of religious education teachers is to be greatly increased, the Act is asking teachers of the subject to be specialists in a far wider area than is the case in other subjects.

To meet this situation a rethinking of the content of teacher training programmes seems indicated. The extension of religious education to respond to religious pluralism has meant that beginner teachers have often found that the information they acquired in their university and college courses enabled them confidently to deal with only part of what the school syllabus prescribed. Courses which dealt with Christian theology were insufficient because they did not help in teaching about non-Christian faiths and the newer religious studies courses were either too generalized or concentrated on one or two religions to the exclusion of the others. Teachers have found it necessary to undertake extensive study and inservice courses to fill in the gaps in their initial training and equip themselves to do justice to demands of the newer agreed syllabuses. Thought needs to be given to what content should be included in university and college courses for those who are going to teach religious education and possibly new degree courses designed for that purpose. The growing number of modularized degree courses may help and prospective religious education teachers would be advised to select those modules which are going to make up the best package for their purpose.

There is the further matter of the number of teachers now required. In the past many schools have quietly dropped religious education except in the lower forms while others have argued that the law did not require religious education for pupils beyond the statutory school leaving age. The new Act makes it clear that the subject must be taught to all pupils irrespective of age, which will involve a much augmented teaching force. Often the subject is now taught by those who are untrained in it, and many who are trained transfer to teaching other subjects after a few years. The problem of how the subject can be staffed with a sufficient number of adequately trained teachers is made more urgent by the new legal provisions. Suggestions have been made, both in the Parliamentary debates prior to the Act, and elsewhere, that there is a reservoir of competent persons, such as clergy and other religious leaders, who can be called in straightaway to fill the gaps; but that ignores the fact that such people, unless they rapidly acquire a different perception of a teacher's rôle and different pedagogical methods from those given them in their clerical training, can be negatively effective. There are no short cuts, and if the aspirations of the Education Reform Act in the field of religious education are to be realized then a substantial rethinking of teacher training will be needed; more time and resources given to it; and an extensive programme of recruitment, inservice training and retraining inaugurated. The prestige and remuneration of the teachers, who have not always been considered to qualify for the higher grades on salary scales, will also have to be reconsidered.

The problem of teacher supply and training is recognised in the DES Circular 3/89, which states that 'the teaching of religious education is a national priority area within the LEA Training Grants Scheme' and that £1 million has been allocated for this in 1988-9 and £1.1 million in 1989- 90[4]. This is to provide for the updating of religious education teachers in recent developments in religious studies, for retraining non-specialist religious education teachers in secondary schools, and for meeting the particular needs of consultant teachers with special responsibility for the subject in primary schools as well as the general needs of primary classroom teachers who have little or no background of the subject. Whether this will be sufficient to meet the extended requirements of the Act can be a matter of doubt, and certainly the retraining will need to be extended beyond the next two years if it is to be anything like adequate.

Sixth forms

Education Reform Act 1988, Section 2, 1a
The Act requires 'religious education for all registered pupils at the school'[5], and the DES Circular 3/89 makes it explicit that 'this includes

those in sixth forms and sixth form colleges, and is not confined to pupils of compulsory school age'[6].

The 1944 Act had been less definite, and the notion that religious education was compulsory only up to the statutory leaving age has led to it being dropped in the upper forms and in the sixth form. In other schools it has been treated flexibly in the sixth form, either being included in an integrated studies or humanities courses, or made one of a number of options. The new requirements are, therefore, going to cause some difficulties. Presumably it can no longer be an option for those who are so inclined and interested, but must be taken by all students. Its inclusion in integrated courses raises a number of problems. How much time must it occupy in such a course to comply with the law? Will it be possible in an integrated course, without doing damage to the aims and balance of the course, to ensure that the religious education component reflects the fact that the religious traditions of Britain are mainly Christian? If the law is to be obeyed strictly in sixth form a good deal of rethinking, rearranging and re-timetabling will be necessary.

At the same time, the extension of the subject to pupils who have reached a more mature stage of thinking could be advantageous. Research into children's religious thinking has shown that to teach them more than simple externals of religious observance at an early age is to risk distorted understanding and that only at a later stage of development is it possible to convey what religion at its best is about. The present custom of confining religious education to the lower forms tends to give the impression that religion is a collection of unusual and arbitrary practices rather than a set of deeply felt beliefs and commitments. The extension of religious education to sixth forms would make it possible to discuss, with pupils who are able to discuss abstractly and objectively, how religious people feel, what is the basis of their beliefs and how the practices express those feelings and beliefs. The sixth formers will not necessarily accept the beliefs they discuss, but they may have a keener insight into them, and that would be a more complete education about religion than many pupils are acquiring at present.

There is, of course, again the question of teacher supply. More teachers will be needed to teach sixth form religious education, particularly in those schools where it has not been taught for some time, and those teachers will need both greater depth of knowledge and the expertise to discuss religion at a deeper level of abstraction than they would frequently have to employ if dealing only with lower forms. The matters of teacher recruitment and of the nature of teacher training for sixth form work will need to be addressed.

In connection with teaching religious education to older pupils the relation of that work to GCSE and other public examinations has to be considered. The newly constructed GCSE syllabuses tend to ask for the study of more than one religion and for each religion studied to have equal importance. If the interpretation of the Act is that Christianity must predominate, how will it square with taking such examinations? Two outcomes are possible: either the examination syllabuses will need to be reformed and Christianity re-established in them as the major study, or, where choice of papers is wide enough, pupils will have to select in such a way as to make sure that they are mainly studying content which is related in some way to Christianity. Since so much thought was given only a few years ago to liberalizing the examination syllabuses this must surely seem regressive. There is the further possibility that if pupils of examination age are required to take a religious education course which complies with the law, but not with the examination syllabus, they will not feel inclined to undertake in addition the further study involved in preparing for the examination, and so numbers taking GCSE Religious Studies will decline. As a way round this difficulty DES Circular 3/89 suggests that SACREs might consider incorporating suitable existing GCSE syllabuses into their local agreed syllabus, or even developing their own GCSE syllabus for that purpose[7]. Nevertheless, it seems a pity that in drawing up the religious provisions of the Act, their likely interaction with examination syllabuses was not more fully taken into account.

Grant-maintained schools

Education Reform Act 1988, Sections 84-88
One of the most innovatory aspects of the 1988 Education Reform Act is that it provides the opportunity for certain schools to detach themselves from the control of the local education authority and have a degree of direct control over the way they arrange their procedures. Any school (apart from primary schools with less than 300 pupils) may apply for this status provided a majority of parents vote for it in a secret ballot. After such a ballot the Secretary of State may agree that the school shall become a 'grant-maintained school', receiving its funding directly from the Department of Education and Science. The governing bodies of these schools are then responsible for the control of how that funding is used, for the provision of a curriculum within the restraints of the Act, and for the good regulation of the schools generally.

   The Act goes to some length to spell out that its religious provisions apply to grant-maintained schools in the same way as they applied before the schools achieved that status. Worship, mainly of a Christian nature, and education reflecting the Christian traditions of the country must take place in them, though where they have been previously called county schools the head may ask the local SACRE for permission for the requirement of Christian worship not to apply to all or part of the school.

In grant-maintained schools that were formerly county schools religious teaching is to be according to 'the appropriate agreed syllabus', with the possibility of some pupils being taught according to the tenets of a particular faith if their parents request it and it can reasonably be provided without extra cost falling on the governing body. Much the same applies to a school that was previously controlled but if parents ask for religious teaching according to a particular faith the governors must, unless it is unreasonable to do so, make that teaching available 'during not more than two periods in each week'[8]. If a voluntary aided or special agreement school becomes grant-maintained the religious education may be in accord with its trust deeds or in accord with what was done before it became aided, but here again parents may ask for agreed syllabus teaching and the governors must provide it in school at the time normally allocated to religious education.

In all grant-maintained schools the syllabus used has to be appropriate. That does not mean that the school can select any existing syllabus that appeals to it. The Act makes it clear that in former county and controlled schools the appropriate syllabus is the one that was used immediately before the school became grant-maintained, which means, in effect, the syllabus adopted by the local authority of the area. Presumably that will be the one used in former aided schools when parents request its use for their children. When an LEA adopts a new syllabus that becomes the appropriate one for grant-maintained schools in its geographical area. Although grant-maintained schools may have one non-voting representative on SACREs, no provision is made for them to be included in Agreed Syllabus Conferences. The Act does, however, state that a Conference reconsidering a syllabus 'shall consult the governing body of the grant-maintained school before making any recommendation'[9]. It is not clear whether this consultation merely concerns the desirability of changing the existing syllabus or whether it permits the grant-maintained schools to express opinions about the content of the syllabus.

On the whole the clauses referring to religious education in grant-maintained schools are intended to tidy up and clarify the position and to make it plainly understood that the legal requirements for religious education and for worship apply to them in the same way as they apply to other schools.

Note on City Technology Colleges

The newly proposed City Technology Colleges are not mentioned in the clauses in the Act relating to religious education and collective worship, and so, presumably, the provisions do not strictly apply to them. There is, however, the possibility that such colleges may be required indirectly to conform. The DES Circular 3/89 gives the information that 'as a condition of grant they will be expected to make provision for religious education and collective worship which is broadly in line with that in maintained schools[10]. This is in accord with Section 105 of the Act, which stipulates that the Secretary of State will make payment to such institutions only if he approves of their broad curriculum; but it raises a nice constitutional point of whether in a matter that evokes such diverse high feelings as religious education, and which the legislators have seen fit to define and control more closely than other subjects, it is entirely appropriate that the Secretary of State should have the power to extend the law to an area not specifically considered in Parliamentary debate.

References

1   *Education Act 1944,* Section 27, 2.

2   Ibid., Section 30.

3   *Education Reform Act 1988,* Section 8, 3.

4   Department of Education and Science (1989), *Circular 3/89; The Education Reform Act 1988: Religious Education and Collective Worship*, Section 56.

5   *Education Reform Act 1988,* Section 2, 1a

6   Department of Education and Science (1989), *Circular 3/89; The Education Reform Act 1988: Religious Education and Collective Worship*, Section 29.

7   Ibid., Section 19

8   *Education Reform Act 1988*, Section 85, 2.

9   Ibid., Section 88, 2.

10   Department of Education and Science (1989), *Circular 3/89; The Education Reform Act 1988; Religious Education and Collective Worship*, Section 70.

Chapter Nine
Religious Education after the 1988 Education Reform Act: Can it Seize the Opportunities?
Josephine M. Cairns

If opportunities were missed by the religious education that followed the 1944 Education Act (as I have argued in Chapter 2), it will be interesting to see whether the clauses of the 1988 Education Reform Act can lead religious educators to grasp those opportunities now available.

Precisely what these opportunities are we must now examine, but perhaps we should consider first the limitations of the situation that has arisen in the period between the two Acts. In the 1988 Hockerill Lecture[1], Clifford Longley points out the chief limitation in his examination of the 'complacent assumptions' which have bedevilled the subject:

> An RE teacher in a secular school in the state sector cannot call upon the ordinary authority of his status in the classroom in order to teach Christianity as true. For he has no mandate. Neither society in general, nor parents in particular, would back him up. Or if they would they have not yet said so.

In other words, Longley is warning us that it is insufficient to present religious truth in England in solely Christian form without first subjecting it to a rational, and perhaps sceptical, analysis. Further limitations are caused by the manner in which religious education has been handled since 1944. In the first place it has been dismissed for its overtly evangelistic aims by an already post-Christian society. Secondly its method of dealing with post-Christian pluralism has led to an over-concentration on an objective and external 'phenomenological' study. As a result, pupils are encouraged to acquire facts about religions rather than to investigate religion in order to relate it to their personal beliefs and development.

It could be that the inability of children to relate the way the subject was presented in schools to their personal spiritual needs has been the principal motivation in rethinking the purpose of religious education, both within the teaching profession and in Parliamentary circles. How religious education teachers respond to their hunch that they have a rôle to play in exercising the spiritual awareness of their pupils will depend, at least in part, on the legislation which the 1988 Act provides. That Act states that it seeks to provide a curriculum that promotes 'the spiritual, moral, cultural, mental and physical development of pupils at the school and of society'[2]. It should follow that a sensitive analysis of the relationship between the culture, mores and spiritual perceptions of a society should underpin any teaching of the young of that society in matters moral, spiritual and cultural. The problem seems to be that the legislation relating to religious education shows little evidence that this relationship has been deeply considered. On the surface the legislators appear to have already established a link between teaching in those three areas and a predominantly Christian content. Could this be, in the long run, another missed opportunity, or is it a valuable and realistic way of promoting explicit education in moral and spiritual matters?

Religious education: spirituality and a secular, plural culture

At the very least the Act invites teachers to discuss openly an educational problem which has grown in significance and proportion over the last 15 years or so; namely, what explicit guidance should be offered to young people about moral and religious ideas and practices in a country which refuses to nominate any one moral code or any one religious philosophy as that to which it is prepared to be committed. There are three aspects to such a culture:

1. It has espoused scientific and evolutionary thinking in such a way that it believes human beings can order and control the universe and their ultimate destiny. This was accurately and effectively described by Clifford Longley in *The Times* on 9 January, 1978:

The basic alteration in human consciousness has been a shift in values and a change in top moral priorities. It could be called anti-Copernican in that it has put man as an individual back into the centre of the universe, no longer a mere particle of the system existing for other purposes, whether divine or scientific.

   The new emphasis is on what it means to be human...The new ideology concentrates on the quality of the experience of human life, in which the quality of relationships is the most important element. A thing is wrong if it feels wrong, in complete reversal of the old morality, which believed in objective 'wrong' which emotions of guilt merely confirmed.[3]

2. Its outlook is thoroughly relativist, which means that it refuses to consider, as Longley has pointed out, absolutes in morality and ultimate questions of truth in matters of religion.
3. It chooses to mask a confusion as to its identity in a pre-occupation with a technological and economic concern for a materially enhanced life style. Further it finds it easier to acknowledge its academic and media-based interest in any life style, religious or otherwise, that presents itself, than to define and recognize the perceptions and values underlying its own.

The inability to define the nature and the roots of the culture of our present society must to some extent be linked with a reticence to articulate the religious sensitivities and attitudes which inform the lives of many British people. In a survey undertaken by the Independent Broadcasting Authority[4] in 1986, 47 per cent of the population said that they would describe themselves as 'very' or 'fairly' religious, and 42 per cent said they were 'certain' that there was a God. Furthermore, 65 per cent thought that religion was a good thing because it provided a set of rules to live by, while 81 per cent saw it as good because it helps people to face problems. Yet the same survey records that only 9 per cent of the population go regularly to church, and the inference must be that there is a strong element of religious belief within the community which does not wish to be tied to liturgical and doctrinal expression. Perhaps these findings lend support to the idea that the community at large would support some initiation of their young into the ideas and beliefs of Christianity because it would help them to be good, but they would not wish them to be full participants in orthodox Christian practice. It is interesting to speculate how they think their children will acquire the basic Christian attitudes without being introduced to the doctrinal teaching which underpins them, and how they think they themselves would have come upon their ideas of God if they had not received such teaching in the past.

Anomie, the individual and the search for cohesion
This refusal to give common expression to deeply held beliefs about the universe and about personal conduct has generated within our culture a heavy burden for individuals who must choose their own life styles and

value systems on their own responsibility and without explicit guidance. This burden was described by a 20 year–old man, currently serving an eight year sentence for robbery and assault, in *The Observer* of 27 November 1988, as follows:

> There is no set of applied rules, no common cause to hold us together, no one to look up to. Each chooses his own way. There is no glue to hold the youth, no sense of belonging to an extended family.[5]

The Prime Minister, Mrs Margaret Thatcher, had commented in not dissimilar vein a month previously:

> Mrs. Thatcher emphasized that 'social cohesion' was not a phrase she ever used. She preferred to talk of the general fabric of the nation, of working together and of neighbourhood. There was still far too much thinking in Britain on the lines of 'I have a problem, the Government must solve it'. It was up to the individual to tackle it first. 'You don't get a responsible nation until you get a nation of responsible citizens. That is the price of freedom.'[6]

The democracy which the Prime Minister describes, where individuals have freedom to be themselves, depends both on the willing co-operation of those individuals to uphold each other's rights and on the young conforming to ideas about freedom and democracy similar to those which their elders hold. Such a process of handing on ideals is intimately bound up with formal education. The ideals which education promoted in the 1970s were those of autonomy and freedom. These permeated curricular activity at all levels, since the aim of education was to develop self-determining individuals who must be given access to each area of knowledge and experience. In this way educators, anxious to avoid imposing their own understandings and values on the young, sought to prepare pupils for living in a still nameless culture by giving them an intellectual passport into their own liberal and rational world.

Indeed it is possible to discern a development in attitudes to individualism during the last half century. It has been argued in Chapter 2 that part of the intention of the 1944 Education Act was to educate individuals to their full potential, but at that time it was still possible to think, as Sir Fred Clarke put it in his *Freedom in the Educative Society*, that 'it is the first business of education to induce conformity in terms of the culture in which the child will grow up'.[7] In the 1970s there was a tacit assumption that the ideal individualism to which education was directed was that of the liberal rationalist, whose attitudes were shaped by intellectual discipline and rigorous discussion. At no time did it seem necessary to consider the consequences of such unlimited individualism either to persons or to society. But there is in the 1980s – a time characterized by increasing violence, by consumerism, and by sometimes aggressive self-assertion – the temptation to posit a connection between undirected individualism and social ills. It may be this that has led the Government, in the Education Reform Act, to call for individual academic excellence in subjects important to the national interest and to appeal to the Christian religious traditions of the country to take hold of, and shape the spiritual and moral persuasions of individual pupils.

Religious education and a confused cultural identity: missing opportunities
This is one possible interpretation of the intentions behind the Act. If it is correct, then we must ask whether the prescription is likely to succeed or whether it is too simplistic. Does it rightly judge the temper of the times, or is it addressing a situation that may have obtained in the past, but does so no longer? Is the 1988 Education Reform Act not proposing a remedy which might have been more appropriate in 1944, but which may have been outdated even then? Will reflecting Christian traditions and indulging in broadly Christian worship have the effect of uniting a multicultural society in which a variety of religious faiths and secular philosophies are held, sometimes deeply? To nominate Christianity in 1944 as the religion to be studied may well have challenged some emerging and half-thought-out secular philosophies to extrapolate and articulate their own justification; in such a way the increasingly educated democracy of Britain might have decided whether it wished to be a post-Christian multi-culture or a Christian culture which welcomed the opportunity to share ideas and insights on morality and spiritual awareness with other faiths. The latter choice is no longer possible in 1988 because, without the benefit of an adequate religious education, society at large has chosen almost unconsciously to divorce itself from orthodox Christianity. The former can be possible only if religious education substantially ignores the prescription to take account of the broad Christian traditions of the country and concentrates instead on questioning life styles and values in a spiritual context which comprises all the religious traditions now established here. It is probably too late to restore the culture completely to Christianity when the majority of its citizens insist on making their religious beliefs and aspirations part only of their private lives. There is a possibility, however, that we might educate for a post-Christian multiculture.

The Act gives the impression that the Government hopes that it will contribute to at least some revival of the Christian culture, despite the fact that its other sections emphasize the diverse cultural nature of the community, and despite the direction of curriculum development in religious education over the last decade or more. That development has encouraged pupils to learn about each other's beliefs and practices while at the same time coming to some conclusion about their own. Thus the Hampshire Agreed Syllabus of 1978 states that:

> Many pupils are engaged in a personal search for meaning, purpose and values. A religious education which is seeking neither to indoctrinate nor to persuade should afford them positive help in the search.[8]

It is possible that the Government recognizes the role of religion in each person's quest for meaning and value and wishes to use the legislation to support the continued work of religious education in assisting pupils to develop fully as physical, moral and spiritual beings. Indeed DES Circular 3/89 explicitly states that:

> The Government believes that all those concerned with religious education should seek to ensure that it promotes respect, understanding and tolerance for those who adhere to different faiths.[9]

Yet it is a matter for speculation whether, as a result of not taking wide enough advice, they have, nevertheless, adopted too narrow a view of the manner in which the religious quest should be conducted in multicultural Britain. By weighting representation on Agreed Syllabus Conferences and on SACREs towards the Christian community they may well have ensured that the resulting religious education will prove too restricted for the majority of pupils to respond to, and from which to find help.

SACREs and syllabuses for the times: the opportunities

Notwithstanding what many regard as over-representation of the Church of England on Syllabus Conferences and SACREs, there is a potential for such bodies to engage in a wide-ranging conversation about, and assessment of, the needs of the schools and pupils in their areas in relation to moral and spiritual development. But they will first need to ask themselves whether they represent adequately the cultural diversity and religious pluralism of the vicinity, thereby causing themselves to be mindful not only of the legal requirements which they must fulfil but also of their role as guardians of such matters. Christians will wonder how they are to affect the moral and spiritual growth of the young in schools when their churches so patently fail to do this, and representatives of other major religions will ask how well their Christian colleagues understand the kind of moral and spiritual development they wish their children to have to ensure that they grow to be adults fully committed in their parents' faith. SACREs and Syllabus Conferences will acknowledge a need to consult with teachers to see how they have gone about such work formerly. Such consultations may prompt SACREs to commission research and encourage thinking about how pupils discover and develop their personal and social attitudes to religion and morality, and the Syllabus Conferences to construct agreed syllabuses which sensitively take account of this research.

Syllabuses of that type might take two forms. The first would concern itself with the religion(s) which most faithfully represents the orthodox spiritual ethos of the neighbourhood. That religion (or those religions) would form the basis of the syllabus whose chief concern would be to enable the pupils to acknowledge and evaluate their own moral and spiritual beliefs in the light of the common tradition(s) into which they had been initiated. The pupils would thus have a model of religion and morality offered to them which was considered important in the whole community. Further, by participating in this tradition they would find that they had experienced a common language and a common symbolism which they might, while living in that community, choose to use to communicate their own moral and spiritual perceptions. The other form of syllabus would result from a Syllabus Conference which was prepared to look more deeply into the religious tensions and diversities of a community and thereby encompass the questions and concerns of young people, growing up in a wider post-Christian and multi-cultural world. Such an analysis would ensure that there was a link established in the syllabus between the problems of the parents and elders of the various religious communities and the aspirations of their children and adolescents who were born here and reared in the Western tradition.

It is difficult at this stage to state in detail what those two types of syllabus would contain, but the first would initiate the pupils into one or two major religious traditions established within a community. It would enable the faith communities to ensure that teaching in state schools is not running counter to the nurture which they themselves are providing. Yet it would allow the school to make clear to all pupils, whether from a religious or a secular home, that it valued orthodox religion in the curriculum as a means of reflecting on and becoming familiar with non- cognitive areas of experience, and the moral and spiritual ideas that may flow from them. The second type of syllabus would have at its core the questions and problems which any community wishing to be coherent faces in our present diverse and plural society. Some of those problems might be how best we organize and consolidate reasonable relationships in our personal and our communal lives; how we define and transmit the sources of authority which we respect; how we regard, respect and treat the created universe; how we impart our spiritual perceptions within a secular and materialist ethos; and how we establish our individual identity in an environment where so many life styles jostle for our attention. A Conference which approached syllabus-making in this way would seek to provide opportunities for the pupils to look behind the outward manifestations of religion to the way in which religions deal with questions provoked by a thoughtful and sensitive approach to living. Both forms of syllabus, skilfully taught, would lead to informed conversation and to some depth of understanding about religion and its place in a plural culture. The second form, however, seems more directly related to the needs of those most specifically multicultural communities in Britain and is better placed to win support for the teaching of religion in a culture which does not define itself as religious.

To look on the provisions of the Education Reform Act as an opportunity to win back our overtly secular culture to its Christian antecedents would be failing the more thoughtful understandings of our times which educationalists, journalists, parents and some politicians have recently proffered. The signs are in fact propitious for changing the way in which we shall, in the near future, choose to describe our culture. Disenchantment with the pressing mechanistic demands of a materialist society seems to be forcing us back to consciousness of the roots of the culture which we currently espouse. In educational circles we have perhaps too thoughtlessly called our culture secular and multicultural and not taken due cognizance of the private religious feelings of many citizens, or of the rôle which the newer faith communities are playing in shaping our social perceptions. The new Act, by charging us to be responsible in the curriculum for the cultural development of our pupils and society, has called attention to the disjuncture which many experience between their private and personal lives and the wider community. This will remain the case until we can share a more precise understanding of a cultural vision which would underpin daily life. In speaking to the 1944 Act, R. A. Butler said:

> The great thing we can feel in passing this Bill is that the structure we have here does violence to no one's conscience, it gives opportunity to everyone's individuality, and upon that structure there can be built a system of education which will make the world a better place, and life a worthier thing.[10]

The religious education that followed the 1944 Education Act did not completely seize that opportunity. It might now be argued that the 1988 Education Reform Act does not always legislate sensitively for the new situation in which education finds itself. Nevertheless, opportunities abound. Will religious education, within the framework of the Act, be able to grasp them? Or will they be missed again?

References

1 Clifford Longley, 'Time for a Fresh Vision' (The 1988 Hockerill Lecture) abridged in *The Times* 19 November 1988.

2 *Education Reform Act 1988,* Section 1, 2a.

3 Clifford Longley, 'What the Churches can offer the new moral ideology', *The Times* 9 January 1978.

4 Independent Broadcasting Authority (1988), *Godwatching: Viewers, Religion and Television*. London: John Libbey.

5 'Behind Bars', *The Observer* 27 November 1988.

6 Robin Oakley (1988), 'Now it's up to the people', *The Times* 26 October 1988.

7 Fred Clarke (1942) *Freedom in the Educative Society*. London: University of London Press.

8 Hampshire Agreed Syllabus, 1978.

9 Department of Education and Science (1989), *Circular 3/89; The Education Reform Act 1988: Religious Education and Collective Worship*, Section 8.

10 R. A. Butler quoted in the Editorial of *Religion in Education*, Vol 11, No. 3, July, 1944.

Chapter Ten
Why Religion?
Edwin Cox

The first section of the 1988 Education Reform Act defines one of the basic purposes of the national curriculum as promoting 'the spiritual, moral, cultural, mental and physical development of pupils at the school and of society.[1] The last three words are especially interesting because they show that the government is concerned not merely with education in its own right but also with the effect that present education is likely to have on society both now and in the future.

Religious education is, then, included in the basic curriculum because it is thought to make some essential contribution to spiritual, moral, cultural and mental well-being, even though it may not greatly affect physical development. It is necessary, therefore, in any overall assessment of the aims and possible outcome of the Act to enquire in what ways the study of religion is thought to be able to influence individuals and society in the desired direction, and whether the content and method of teaching envisaged is going to have the desired effect, given the existing intellectual climate and the function that religions play in a pluralistic culture. To put it bluntly, what are the religious provisions of the Act intended to accomplish? Why is religion included in the curriculum at all? Will religious education, as defined in the Act, be able to make an effective contribution to personal growth and social well-being?

It is easy, taking a cavalier and superficial view, to find many causes for thinking that the religious clauses of the Act are unsatisfactory, a number of which have been pointed out in other parts of this book. If the 1944 Act legislated for a religious situation that was already passing and the 1988 Act is trying to reiterate its provisions, without regard to the changes that have occurred in the intervening 44 years, then the new provisions are even more unrealistic and likely to be equally ineffective. There has been some adverse reaction, even in religious education circles, to the distinctive mention of Christianity, which is seen not as a recognition of an existing social state but as an attempt to give that religion prior status. Moreover, one can get the impression from the cursory reference to them, that the Government has not treated other religious traditions with total seriousness but has hoped that, with predominantly Christian teaching in schools, they will eventually go away. The authors of the Act seem to have had scant understanding of the practical problems of providing worship in schools that has any depth of meaning for the participants, or of the logistic problems that re-establishing a recognizable religious education in the upper school forms is going to cause. Nor is there recognition of the difficulties of teaching about religion to the adolescents of the secular affluent society. One can understand this latter blind spot in politicians. They are accustomed to having their enactments generally realized, and have means of ensuring that their laws have the desired outcome. Being practitioners of the art of the possible, they do not usually pass laws that cannot be enforced. They seem however to be myopic when it come to education, and imagine that to require a thing to be taught means that it will, as a matter of course, be learned and accepted. This ignores that unpredictable ingredient in education, which requires (and perhaps particularly in religious education) a favourable attitude and co-operative spirit in the pupils. Because of all these considerations it may be doubtful whether the religious clauses in the new Act are going to make a significant difference to what goes on in schools, or help solve the problems with which religious education has been struggling in the past.

This catalogue of reservations may, however be too sweeping, and so superficial as to miss the point. Politicians may have some clouding of vision when dealing with education but they are not entirely without perception. They, and their advisers at the DES, cannot have made an Act as inappropriate as the preceding paragraph suggests. Clumsy it may be, but surely there must be some defensible purpose behind it, which does not explicitly appear from reading the Act itself. So what deeper aim had the legislators in the back of their minds when passing the religious clauses of the 1988 Act? What further personal and social good do they hope will emerge from a revitalized religious education?

Before addressing that question, comment has to be made on how religious education appears to have been considered in the Parliamentary debates on the Education Reform Bill. The majority of speakers seem to have assumed that the purpose of religious education is to make pupils religious in some way, or to help them to be more religious than they already are. The educational approach to religion, as something to be learned about as an important aspect of human behaviour, and to be assessed impartially as a result of that learning, did not often surface. The debates, therefore, had the emotional and evangelistic tinge that so often accompanies discussion of religion, and the subsequent Act may have been affected accordingly. It was not debated in educational terms and that may explain why some of its demands seem educationally difficult, if not unrealistic.

To return to the consideration of the possible underlying purposes of the religious education provisions, there are four that seem worth reviewing.

To promote religious belief?
Amplifying the view expressed above that many supporters of the Act saw it as propagating religion, one can quote examples from their speeches in Parliament, particularly in the House of Lords. For instance Lord Jakobovits, the Chief Rabbi, said, 'Religious education must be a transmission of a commitment even more than of mere knowledge'[2]; and Lord Elton was of the opinion that young people's 'understanding of life will be impaired if they do not receive some instruction in the religion of their country'[3]. If this is what the Act is intended to facilitate it goes further than the Spens Report of 1938[4] which said that in order to be educated it is necessary to be aware of the fact of a religious view of life. The argument now seems to be that religion is a good and necessary thing to have, and that pupils are not merely to be made aware of a religious attitude but actually be given, or be encouraged to adopt, that attitude. The requirements for daily worship reinforce this interpretation of the Act's intention, since that presumes that pupils will not only be taught about religion but also made sufficiently responsive to it to be able to practise it in the worship sessions.

The argument here seems to be that religion in some conscious and structured form is an essential part of human experience, which is defective without it. All cultures have up to the present had their religions and when, as in the latter stages of the Roman Empire, the religion decays then the culture decays with it. Our existing culture needs a religious underpinning for it to flourish and continue. Churches and homes are failing in their duty to teach all children a religious faith and so something must be done in schools to make good the deficiency. Against this it is possible to point out that in the present century some countries have tried, with varying success, deliberately to eradicate religion: in the United States of America, where religion is more evident than in Britain, teaching of it in schools is illegal; religion in this country is no longer taken into account by many in deciding their life styles; and – apart from some formal religious observances which are mostly undergone as a matter of course – religion does not affect politics, economic decisions, industry and commerce, sport or most social occasions. Because of the effect on human thinking of the discoveries of the last two centuries, making humans more pragmatically and less imaginatively minded than before, religion affects the culture less because it has become a matter of private choice. As Paul Hirst has pointed out:

> In so far as religious and non-religious people can agree about social principles, religious questions can be regarded as a personal private matter... Such privatization is increasingly the mark of our society, in which the widest range of attitudes to religious beliefs is acceptable, provided they are never allowed to determine public issues.[5]

If Hirst is right, then it is difficult to justify trying to propagate religion of any kind in county schools. That is the proper task of the religious bodies themselves and of parents rather than a state educational system. If, however, it is the intention of the Act that religious education shall make children religious, albeit in a liberal and pluralistic manner, it implies that the legislators think that the welfare of society requires that religion be rescued from privatization and re-established as an influence in communal decisions. It is not intended here to discuss whether this is a valid view, but merely to point out that the framers of the Act may have based their decisions on an incomplete analysis of the function of religion in British culture at the end of the twentieth century, and some of the practical difficulties of implementing the legislation may spring from that fact.

To teach morality?
The British have always been inclined to Pelagianism and to emphasize the moral aspects of religion rather than the doctrinal and ecclesiastical. Parents who are themselves little influenced by a religious outlook, but subscribe to Matthew Arnold's definition of religion as 'morality tinged with emotion', often support religious education on the grounds that at least it will make their children good. Parliamentary speeches in support of the Act frequently give the impression that moral training is the reason for including religious education in the curriculum. For instance Lord St. John said:

> What is important is that the religious foundation of morality should be maintained. It was the 17th century which coined an aphorism, 'No Bishop, no King'. Our own could coin another. 'No religion, no morality', and certainly

history affords no example of a society which has permanently maintained morality without a religious basis.[6]

And when Lord Houghton asked of the Bill being debated:

> What is the aim? Is the aim morality, which is so frequently mentioned, or is it belief? Do we not want better behaviour from our children rather than a belief in an almighty being? Must we teach them religion in order to achieve some concept of morality, human relationship, affection and understanding?[7]

Hansard reports that his peers answered with a spontaneous 'Yes'. This gives the impression that religion is to be taught, not for its own sake, but because of the morality that will flow from it.

This ignores the fact that religious education, as it has previously been taught, has not had a strongly moral effect, though that may be because of the way it has been taught, and it might have stronger moral influence if taught differently in the future. It also ignores philosophical attempts to establish a basis for morality on rational and empirical grounds, independent of a transcendental belief system, and the curriculum development work that has been done to fashion a moral education programme that will operate independently of pupils' religious commitments. Nor does it totally take into account the possibility that, though morality may ultimately spring from people's deep responses to what is considered to be true and real and of overriding importance, many do not now find it necessary to connect those responses with religious doctrines and practices, or to talk of them in the language of religion. It goes beyond the scope of this book to discuss the relationship of morality and religion, but the matter is raised to pose the question of whether, if the intention of the Act is to elicit 'better behaviour from our children', the philosophical implications and the pragmatic difficulties of implementation have been considered as profoundly as they might have been.

To promote social consensus?

It is not impossible that behind the Act there was the wider and vaguely felt purpose of bringing some consensus and cohesion to a society that, because of the rapid changes it has undergone, has lost its sense of direction. This is to some extent speculative, but it is perhaps justified by the statement that education is concerned with the 'development of pupils at the school and of society'[1], which implies that it is intended to do some good to society as well as to the individual.

As more fully discussed in Chapter 2, this was of particular concern at the time of the 1944 Education Act, when religious education was thought able to make a major contribution to social cohesion. That concern was articulated in a leader in *The Times Educational Supplement* of 30 October 1944, which said that:

> What is of vital importance to the nation at the moment is the lack of and need for a unifying philosophy or general conception of life. The previously accepted conception is clearly disintegrating and is moreover assailed by contrary conceptions... In these circumstances it is essential to undergird the national system of education with some unifying purpose[8].

Since that time British society has become even more diverse. Rapid travel and migration has led to a mingling of cultures all over the world, which has brought not only an enrichment of experience but also a new set of tensions. Greater freedom of individual thought and action has led to widening horizons and extended opportunities for fuller life styles, but also to the possibility of those opportunities being mishandled. There has been a lessening of a sense of an authority structure which gives cohesion to a society, with the result that individual freedom becomes unbounded and open to misuse. Consequently although our society has become more varied and richer it is subject to pressure at the seams. Terrorism, increasing and more violent crime, aggressive personal aggrandizement which scorns the needs of others, and pressure group action which takes little heed of its effect on the remainder of the population, the ready resort to drugs heedless of the hygienic consequences, are signs of the strains of our culture and are causing more than a little concern to thoughtful people. The problem is how to preserve the new richness and freedom that a liberal multiculture has won without resorting to an oppressive and stultifying authoritarianism. How can it be assured that the richness and freedom will be enjoyed constructively and not be so misused as to destroy themselves in anarchy? For that, society needs an agreement on what values it will respect, what kind of life the individual can aim to achieve without detriment to neighbours, and a voluntary acceptance of the boundaries between a liberating freedom and diversity on the one hand and a destructive anarchy on the other.

For such a moral consensus to arise there is a need for an educated vision of the possibilities both of the individual and of society and a willingness to realize that vision. The Education Reform Act may be part of the government's concern with creating such a consensus, which is why it included in the Act not only the vocational training it thinks the country needs but also the spiritual and moral development of society. The problem is that we have minimum experience of how to create such a vision in a secular culture. Most consensual visions in the past have resulted from religious systems, and where the religious systems have broken down moral disintegration has tended to occur. That is not to say a secular moral consensus is impossible, but the Act seems to assume that the quickest way to arrive at a consensus is by a religious education that recalls British Christian traditions.

Wise and desirable though it may be to seek a consensus that will alleviate some of the strains on a multicultural society in an age of rapid technological and ethnic change, can it be accomplished by attempting to recreate a Christian vision that served well in the past but has shown signs of decreasing effectiveness in the present century? Or will it be necessary to take a wider view and to appeal as well to other visions that people have, both religious and secular, and try to find what they have in common? Is it possible to arrive at a shared vision without asking particular groups to modify what seems to them of ultimate importance? If it is, then the emphasis on Christianity in the Act begins to look misjudged and even oppressive.

A more genuine consensus might be achieved by finding agreement on what the many religions and other ultimate philosophies have in common. This would mean asking what it is that people are seeking in religious and philosophical ideas, why they resort to them at all, and what assurance, confidence and assessment of life's values they find in them. There might be a basis of consensus here if everyone is reaching out for the same things, even though the ways in which they describe their search and their conclusions are conditioned by their cultural backgrounds and therefore often appear on the surface to be diverse. An education dealing with belief systems which was founded on this outlook could include a sympathetic study of a range of religions and secular beliefs (and a critical discussion of them with older pupils). Though more complex and less amenable to instant results, such a study would escape the charge of apparent indoctrinational intention and, in the long run, might bring a united vision of how the present multiculture could find coherence and mutual respect without sacrificing its multifarious richness.

To provide for transcendental experience?

Though there is not as much as a hint of it in the wording of the Act, there may be a deeper 'hunch' (no more than that) which influences the British, both elected Government and electors, to feel the need of some kind of teaching in schools about what is imprecisely called 'the spiritual'. That hunch is that there is more to reality than appears on the surface of the universe. This may account for the recent survey which found that while less than 10 per cent of the population take part in regular religious observance, 56 per cent thought religion necessary and 54 per cent deemed it essential[9]. Those figures show a decline from those of previous surveys, but witness the persistence of an underlying religiosity. Although Britain, in the third quarter of the twentieth century, is outwardly concerned with a thorough-going practical approach to life – seeking industrial efficiency and financial success, applauding the empirical in science and philosophy, admiring a life style that is unashamedly hedonistic, and suspicious of the traditionally cultural and aesthetic – life experience, with its precariousness and its brevity, forces on the individual the occasional thought that there must be more to it than a barren efficiency of getting and spending, of acquiring and using, and that perhaps behind it there is a significance deeper than the physical, a point more profound than transient personal pleasure. In such a mood there is a willingness to admit that we ought not to bring up children without giving them at least a glimpse of the possibility of a transcendent view of life and its purpose.

Related to this are the findings of a number of recent investigations that experiences in which individuals feel that they have come into contact, or at least have had a brush with, the transcendent are far from uncommon[10]. Whether those experiences are interpreted in a religious light or not depends on the assumptions that the experiencers bring to them[11]. Religious people find in them a confirmation of their beliefs, but others describe them in non-theistic terms, frequently in aesthetic ones. Such experiences appear to be the inspirations of art in all its forms, but they can be reacted to in other ways. Maslow, who called them 'peak' experiences rather than transcendent ones, thought they included moments of scientific discovery and intellectual insight, and also moments of athletic achievement.[12]

If moments of transcendental awareness are a common part of the human experience, something that has to be taken into account in assessing what life is about and in planning one's life style, then provision has to be made for them in the educational process. That would justify the inclusion of religious education in the curriculum, but would not justify confining the study to religions alone, much less to one religion. That some people react to transcendental experiences in non-religious ways would necessitate extending the teaching to include consideration of those ways. Religious education, seriously conducted, would be part of the study, but it would widen its borders and make contact with other curriculum

subjects which make possible transcendental experiences or which intro-
duce children to the ways in which artists of all sorts have responded to
those experiences and encapsulated them in their art forms. [13]

If this is what the Act means when it speaks of spiritual development,
then there is justification for including the study of the transcendental
experiences of religion in the curriculum. If, however, it assumes that only
religious transcendental experiences (and specifically Christian ones) are
to qualify, then one has to query whether the legislators have failed to
appreciate the diversity of what needs to be studied and set their bounds
too narrowly.

The debate continues
Although it seems to have been intended to define religious education and
to set it on a well charted course for the immediate future, the ambiguity of
some of the clauses of the Act, and its failure to be based on a satisfactorily
thought-out rationale, means that discussion of what the subject is, and
what it is intended to achieve, is likely to continue. The faith communities
have reacted to it in conflicting ways. Aggressive and militant Christians
have tended to see it as a manifesto for the re-Christianizing of Britain, and
will doubtless try to bring influence to bear, by obtaining representation on
Syllabus Conferences and SACREs, and possibly even by court action on
occasions, to see that it is so interpreted. The greater number of
Christians, however, who think that their faith not only permits, but rather
demands, respect for other sincerely held views, have expressed misgivings about the wisdom of giving such prominence to the Christian religion
and the almost off-hand treatment of other faiths. The secular response
has been more muted than it would have been 20 years ago. Followers of
other religions, particularly Islam, are worried because they fear that their
children will be subjected to influences in school, too strong for home
teaching and example to counteract, which will incline them to abandon
the family religion and become Christian; they interpret the intentions of
the Act in the same way as the militant Christians and would have
preferred a definite statement that their children would be taught their
own particular faith in schools. Many engaged in teaching the subject,
knowing the aggressively unfavourable attitudes that many adolescents
have towards any form of religion, wishing nevertheless to prepare their
pupils for a multicultural world, and sensitive to the danger of being
accused of indoctrination, not only are confused about what they re being
asked to do, but also fear that they may have strong misgivings about it.

There is a certain ambivalence about the religious clauses of the Act which make it difficult to see clearly how they can be entirely implemented. That ambivalence probably springs from the nature of Parliamentary procedure. When the clauses were debated there were those who wished the religious education and worship to be patently Christian, while others looked to it to take more account of multiculture and religious pluralism. Both sides seem to have had their effect on different phrases in the Act, which consequently borders on the ambiguous. For instance, it stipulates collective worship that is mainly and broadly Christian, while taking into account the family backgrounds of the pupils. There will be many schools where to comply with both requirements will need subtle thought. Furthermore the agreed syllabuses are to stress the Christian nature of British religious traditions and take account of other practices. The DES Circular 3/89 (in perhaps a belated attempt to assuage some of the fears of non-Christian bodies) strengthens the latter demand when it affirms that 'the Government believes that all those concerned with religious education should seek to ensure that it promotes respect, understanding and tolerance for those who adhere to different faiths'[14]. These differences, though perhaps not irreconcilable, leave a degree of uncertainty as to what precise form of religious education is being legislated for, and much hard thinking is likely still to be required as to how the subject can obey the law and still contribute to the education of the children of present day Britain.

Whether the Act will greatly change what is done in schools with regard to religious education, or whether practical and pedagogical considerations will cause it to be no more heeded than the provisions of the 1944 Education Act have been in the recent past, can be found only by experience. Clifford Longley may well have been right when he said, in the 1988 Hockerill Lecture:

The real Great Debate about religious education is still only just beginning.[15]

References

1 *Education Reform Act 1988,* Section 1, 2a.

2 *Parliamentary Debates (Hansard),* Vol. 496, No. 120, p. 419.

3 Ibid. p. 424.

4 Board of Education (1938), *Secondary Education with special reference to Grammar School and Technical High Schools* (The Spens Report). London: HMSO.

5 Hirst, P. H. (1974), *Moral Education in a Secular Society*. London: Hodder and Stoughton, p.3.

6 *Parliamentary Debates (Hansard)*, Vol. 496, No. 120, p. 417.

7 Ibid. p. 424.

8 *Times Educational Supplement* leader, 30 October 1944.

9 Independent Broadcasting Authority (1988), *Godwatching: Viewers, Religion and Television*. London: John Libbey.

10 Hay, D. (1987), *Exploring Inner Space*. London: Mowbrays Press; Paffard, M. (1973), *Inglorious Wordsworths*. London: Hodder and Stoughton; Robinson E. and Jackson M. (1987), *Religion and Values at 16+*. London: Christian Education Movement.

11 Cox, E. (1987), 'The Relation Between Belief and Values', *Religious Education*, Vol. 82, pp.12-13.

12 Maslow, A. H.(1964), *Religions, Values and Peak Experiences*. Ohio State University Press.

13 Cox, E. (1987) *Op.cit.*, pp. 16-17.

14 Department of Education and Science (1989), *Circular 3/89; The Education Reform Act 1988: Religious Education and Collective Worship*, Section 8.

15 Longley, C. (1988), 'Time for a fresh vision' (Hockerill Lecture, 1988), abridged in *The Times*, 19 November.

Appendix
Responses from Individuals Within Certain Life Stances

A Christian response

Jean Walker

Christian response to the Act, and particularly to its religious provisions, has been as varied as the groups and individuals within the Christian community. Some responses appear to have been as much a reaction to inaccurate press reporting and wishful thinking as to familiarity with the Act or Circular 3/89 (January 1989) on religious education and collective worship that followed it.

For many Christians there is an air of unreality about much of this legislation. We live in a period of increasing ecumenical co-operation, yet the Act puts the Church of England back into solitary Establishment state on SACREs and Statutory Conferences. We are increasingly involved in dialogue with people of other faith – and SACREs explicitly involve believers in faith other than Christian in their structures – and yet worship is to be 'wholly or mainly of a broadly Christian character'. There is greater freedom in the classroom for the teaching of religious education, in that future agreed syllabuses, while reflecting that our traditions in Britain are mainly Christian, must also take account of the teaching and practice of the other principal religions around us. There seems to be some confusion here between encouragement of good religious education and the preservation of a national heritage. Failings in these areas in the past are due as much to the low status of religious education as to any malign intent or deliberate neglect; simple legislation will not change this.

This confusion was and is apparent in much of the debate. Religion is seen as undergirding moral standards, yet for any individual, morality springs from a total philosophy – or theology – of living. Imposed morality, whatever its source, will not be permanent unless it springs from a personal faith or stance for living.

Christians welcome the statement that a broad and balanced education must include the development of the moral and the spiritual. We welcome the visibility given to religion in the Act. We are forced to note, however, that while the core and foundation curriculum will be funded and resourced in a number of new ways over the next few years, religious education, as a basic curriculum, will again be left to the goodwill of LEAs and schools. The circumstances which led to its substantial neglect in the past will be perpetuated. The status of any subject is proportional to the money, staffing and resources given to it; those are the things that count in the staff-room and in places where budgets and timetabling are decided. Resources are the measure of goodwill and real intent. The DES Circular 3/89 makes many positive and useful suggestions as to how the intentions of the Act are to be carried forward – but all depends on staffing, funding, a commitment to inservice courses for teachers and an intention to take seriously the religious dimensions of initial teacher training.

Many Christians will regret that there has been no positive inclusion of those of other faith with regard to the act of worship. The Act is couched in very broad terms. Recognizing that not every act of worship need be Christian, and that all faiths hold in common many attitudes to the great human virtues and duties, it may be that, with great sensitivity and understanding of each other's needs, Christians and believers of other faith will be able to provide, within the Act's own terms, for all children and their spiritual growth.

The emphasis on the Christian element in religious education must lead to a new awareness of Christianity as a multicultural and multi-ethnic faith. With a world heritage of tradition, history and custom based on common creeds and scriptures, Britain's Christian heritage will be seen as a small part of a greater and much richer whole.

The disappearance of the term 'instruction' with regard to religion in school makes clear the educational dimension increasingly emphasized in recent years. Religious Education as a discrete subject may lead curriculum work, but religious dimensions are present in a greater or lesser degree across the curriculum. This must be understood if pupils are to make sense of their world.

The greatest misgivings are with regard to the act of worship. The fact that over the years most schools have come to use the term 'assembly' for the gathering together of the school to consider things of worth reflects the unease of teachers, Christians and others, in asking children, uncommitted as believers and often from homes with no religious view of life, to 'worship' together. Worship is a major part of the experience of committed believers of all faiths; similar profound experiences are shared by many who would not call themselves believers in a theistic sense. The ability to worship – and indeed to develop religion – is a unique human characteristic. Christian and other believers will not wish to see presented in schools as 'worship' something which may detract from a great human experience. The most we can do in the school assembly is to explore and develop, using the resources of our religious heritage, the skills and experiences which may lead to the threshold of worship for the believer and the non-believer alike. Awe and wonder, the use of silence and meditative thought, the encouragement of empathy, compassion and the sharing of experience, the explorative use of the creative arts and of rituals, to express profound feeling – these are all necessary for the growth of the spiritual dimension in each individual child.

Similarly, religious concepts, the meanings of life, existence and death, the idea of God, the problems of joy and suffering, can be explored in the classroom. Good assemblies have always offered these opportunities. Such assemblies need careful planning and time; whether 'assembling together' of a high quality can be maintained on a daily basis is doubtful. We do not ask ministers of religion to provide acts of worship every day for non-adherents. Most Christian clergy find Sundays quite enough to provide for. Heads with little theological training and little acquaintance with religious philosophies may well feel daunted. Many heads and teachers, too, will feel that professional demands must take precedence over personal conscience in this regard. This can hardly be the right way to bring children to the threshold of worship – to one of the greatest of all human experiences.

The primary concern, now that the Act is a fact of life, should be to assist teachers to work as flexibly as possible within its structures.

The requirement upon local authorities to set up SACREs can give Christian churches a positive opportunity to show their support for schools in the maintained sector. Church representatives who have been involved with SACREs in the past have valued the opportunities they provide to make friendships across the religious and community divides, and to understand more fully the nature of religious education and what it can contribute to education as a whole. This may prove to be the most positive and creative area of the legislation.

Whatever we may feel about its deficiencies or its values, the Act is with us, and Christians will do their best to work constructively within it.

A Hindu response

V. P. (Hemant) Kanitkar

Unlike most other world religions, Hinduism does not provide a structured, formal, creed-based type of religious education for its young
people. The values and practices of the religion are passed on within the
family circle and through participant observation of rituals, festivals,
pilgrimages, etc., hence the wide divergence of belief and practice from
region to region. In modern India no religious instruction is provided in
state schools, in spite of the fact that Hindus form far and away the largest
religious group. There are valid political and historic justifications for this,
but there is also the fact that formalized curriculum-based religious
instruction is not customary for the dominant Hindu group. For such
religions as Islam and Christianity, which have a more structured approach
to religious education, specialized schools and colleges, as well as mosques
and churches, serve the purpose in the 'secular' state that is modern India.

The situation of British Hindus is very different from that of their co-
religionists in India. Their beliefs and rituals do not surround them both
inside and outside the home from an early age, so that they can be
absorbed through a kind of osmosis. The grandparent generation, source
of so many legends and parables, is often absent, left behind in India, and
parents are too busy with jobs and businesses to take time to instruct their
children. Young Hindus see around them the signs of Christian festivals,
and begin to use them as reference points, e.g. 'Diwali is our Christmas' – a
betrayal of understanding of both festivals.

Since young British Hindus are accustomed to the incorporation of
religious education in the school curriculum, it is appropriate that
provision should be made for the teaching of Hinduism, and the Education
Reform Act 1988 does this. It is also right that young Hindus should be
knowledgeable about the society in which they live, characterized as it is
by a Christian-based value system, and this kind of understanding, too, it is
right for schools to provide, as laid down in the 1988 Education Reform
Act, which stresses the preparation of children for adult life.[1]

Some provisions of the Act need clarifying comment, especially where
multi-faith assemblies are concerned. There are many schools in Britain
which have only a few pupils who are definitely not Christian. The parents
of such pupils have a right to withdraw them from the 'collective worship'
and the 'RE lessons' and make other suitable arrangement, provided that
the county school is not expected to bear the expenses of such arrangements. In some areas, such as Greater London and the Midlands, where

there is a large non-Christian population, many schools have a very high percentage of pupils who are not Christian. In such schools the head-teacher, at his or her discretion is empowered to determine the nature of the collective worship.[2] Quite rightly, religious education in such schools *must* be provided by the authorized members of staff and not by any '*outsiders*' whatever their proficiency.

As a Hindu who feels that British-born Hindu children should receive some religious instruction in their faith to enable them to achieve cultural identity *and* social integration, I see no difficulty placed in the way of that objective by this Education Reform Act 1988.

It is the concern of *all teachers* of religious education in England and Wales, aided by inservice courses and facilities at Teachers' Centres, to carry out their duties and exercise their discretion as provided by this Act, to foster and support the *multicultural* nature of British society.

References

1 *Education Reform Act 1988,* Section 1, 2, b.

2 Ibid., Section 12

A Humanist response

John White

'Harmonizers and polarizers'

I have been the Humanist representative on the Inner London Education Authority's Standing Advisory Council on Religious Education for 16 years. I am its longest-serving member – and as there are few SACREs in other authorities this seems to mean that I am probably the longest-serving SACRE member in the country! I have also been an active member of the Religious Education Council and the Standing Conference on Inter-Faith Dialogue in Education for 15 years. It has been an enriching experience and one that has enabled me to 'stand in other peoples' shoes' (to quote that excellent aim from the Hampshire Religious Education Agreed Syllabus). One of the many friends I have made on those bodies is that wise man of vision, Rabbi Hugo Gryn. In a television programme about his life and work he said, 'In my view, the world is divided into *harmonizers* and *polarizers;* this essential difference of outlook transcends all conventional divisions of politics, religion and class.'

For the past 20 years I, and my colleagues in the Humanist movement such as Harold Blackham and James Hemming, have worked in constructive dialogue with 'harmonizers' from all the world life stances. As Humanists, we have advocated the nourishing of that harmonizing process in our schools. Firstly, we have worked for assemblies of the school community that celebrate the moral principles held by all people of goodwill; those basic values that lie at the heart of all societies and civilizations. Secondly, we have wanted to see help given to *all* our pupils to understand and respect the different life stances that people follow and which give their lives meaning and purpose. Education of this kind, we believe, assists each pupil to come to a personal life stance which provides guidance, self-confidence and vision.

The movement towards consensus

I have been heartened to see the extent of the consensus that has emerged. When the Hampshire Agreed Syllabus appeared in 1978 it was adopted in a short time by many other authorities, making it the most widely-used syllabus in the country. Syllabuses with a similar breadth of viewpoint have appeared from areas as different as Manchester, Essex and Inner London.

A spate of documents on assemblies and worship has borne testimony to the vigour of the reappraisal that has occurred[1]. The ILEA publication *Assemblies in County Schools* (1978) sums up much of this thinking; it commends assemblies that encourage all present to think about ultimate values and beliefs, to explore the depths of human relationships or to foster a sense of belonging to a community which strives to achieve the highest standards in all aspects of life.[2]

Worship: the problem of legislation

Considerable harmony of viewpoint has emerged over the *themes* on which assemblies should centre. The ideas advanced in the Hampshire Agreed Syllabus Handbook are similar to those suggested by James Hemming in *Wider Horizons*[3]: 'courage, love, achievement, compassion, wonder, imagination, joy, tragedy, hope, responsibility, humanitarian endeavour, and the mystery of existence'.

However, similar agreement cannot be found over the *assumptions* that underlie worship (in the sense understood by a body of religious believers). Quite apart from the obvious differing theological beliefs that separate the varied practices of Christians, Muslims, Sikhs and Hindus, there is also the problem that Buddhists, Jains and Humanists cannot accept the assumption that a deity exists to be worshipped. Passing an Act of Parliament does not remove these serious difficulties. It places teachers in an impossible position. It also devalues the significance of genuine worship by a faith community.

The concept of 'worth-ship'

These inseparable problems have been discussed now for 20 years. Schools have been seeking a positive way forward in a variety of imaginative ways, particularly in developing a concept of worship as being 'worth-ship' (justified by its Anglo-Saxon root *weorth-scipe*). Assemblies have focused on identifying and celebrating those values of worth within the school community.

They have also been exploring the concept of 'a quiet time'. I remember clearly the complete change of attitude of the students in the London secondary school, in which I taught, when a new headteacher arrived. He immediately abandoned his predecessor's coercion to sing hymns (resulting in the reluctant dismal dirge so well described in the novel *Kes*[4]). Instead, a theme of world or national interest was used as a focus; questions were posed; values were teased out; and then there was a period of quiet to give opportunities for each person present to respond individually – with reflection, meditation or private prayer. Thus the term 'collective worship' was given its full and true meaning – a collection of diverse individuals from a multi-belief, multicultural society, each sensitively drawn to an experience of significance and worth.

The Education Reform Act 1988: worship
But now, alas, an Act is on the Statute Book which (in respect of assemblies and worship) completely ignores all the thoughtful, constructive, *educational* initiatives that were the product of the years of patient dialogue. Little wonder that *The Guardian*[5] commented:

> Perversely, in a world which has become smaller and in a country that now has many faiths, schools are required to become more sectarian. The change runs counter to the facts, much church opinion and the Government's own inspectors' advice.

The reactions of the education profession are reflected in the headlines in the national press: 'Forced to Pray'; 'Prayers Should Not Be Imposed'; 'The Threat to a Fragile Multi-Faith Way'; 'Holy Orders'; 'Onward Christian Soldiers'.

I view this illogical, unexpected rejection of educational opinion with dismay – and that dismay is, I know, shared by many other 'harmonizers', theistic believers and agnostics alike. Our efforts, over so long a period, have been contemptuously brushed aside. Teachers are baffled by this meaningless reversion to nineteenth-century attitudes. There is talk in many schools of every teacher deciding to opt out of school worship.

The Education Reform Act 1988: religious education
There is a small crumb of comfort to be found. This is that the clauses relating to religious education now require that 'account be taken of the teaching and practices of the other principal religious traditions represented in Great Britain'. However, while Humanists welcome this belated widening of scope, they regret that its wording does not acknowledge the widely-held view that if religious education is to grapple honestly with ultimate questions, it must include non-theistic responses such as Buddhism and Humanism. I fear that narrow interpretations of the word 'religious' may further turn back the educational clock.

The democratic process
A final word. As a Humanist, I wish to see an open society which generates a vigorous and responsive democratic process. The *manner* in which these clauses became law gives me deep cause for concern. They were brought forward by a small reactionary pressure group, late at night, in a thinly-attended House of Lords. As soon as they were made known, they were opposed by the teaching unions, the Religious Education Council, and many faith communities. However, we now find them imposed on five million children and half a million teachers. The polarizers have won an important (but, it is to be hoped, temporary) victory.

References

1 Hull, J. (1974) *School Worship: An Obituary*. London: SCM Press.
  Schools Council Working Paper 36 (1971) *Religious Education in Secondary Schools*. London: Evans/Methuen Educational.
  Schools Council Working Paper 44 (1972) *Religious Education in Primary Schools*. London: Evans/Methuen Educational.
  School Morality Council (1970) *Moral and Religious Education in County Schools*. (*ed* H. J. Blackman). London: Social Morality Council.
  Social Morality Council (1976) *Moral and Religious Education in County Primary Schools*. (*ed* H. J. Blackman). Windsor: NFER Publications.
  Free Church Federal Council (1976) *Religious Education in County Schools: A Discussion Document*. London: Free Church Federal Council.

2 ILEA (1978) *Assemblies in County Schools*.

3 Hemming, James (1972) *Wider Horizons*. London: British Humanist Association.

4 Hinds, B. (1969) *Kestrel for a Knave*. Harmondsworth: Penguin Books. (*Kes* is the title of the film.)

5 *Guardian* (30 September, 1988).

A Jewish response

Alastair Falk

Whether assemblies were 'broadly Christian' or narrowly Christian during my own secondary schooling I could not say. Assembly was a time to be spent in a classroom catching up on homework with the help of a tiny handful of Jewish boys who attended the school in Sheffield where I started out. When we later moved to London I found that assemblies were again a time for withdrawal. This time, however, the very large percentage of Jewish boys had led to an arrangement for 'Jewish assemblies' organized by the boys themselves under the general aegis of the only Jewish member of staff, who had presumably had this thankless task thrust upon him.

R.E. (or was it R.K. in those days?) was a different matter. In Sheffield, the small numbers involved meant all Jewish children had to simply slot into another lesson with a different group. I thus became the apple of the Technical Drawing master's eye, since I seemed to be such an enthusiastic attender, appearing in his lessons twice as much as anyone else. In London, on the other hand, the numbers in each class were so large that we simply 'sat and got on with our own work quietly' in the class where the R.E. lesson was taking place. This, of course, left most conscientious R.E. teachers in a dilemma – to ignore or not to ignore; to 'engage in meaningful dialogue' or to 'respect minority sensibilities'.

I mention these experiences to remind readers that this is, as it were, a view from without. It is, however, a view that will again become a common pattern in the post 1988 era if, indeed, it has really ever been any different. Certainly most Jewish parents in my experience show a greater sensitivity to the fear of 'Christian indoctrination' than a commitment to a multi-cultural education. From a minority point of view this is understandable – even a minority as established and as internally pluralistic as the Jews. It is the 'Christian' rather than the 'broadly Christian character' which is likely to be more obvious to Jewish readers of the new legislation – indeed, to most religious minorities something is either Christian or not, the adjectives are irrelevant.

It would seem likely, therefore, that the real effect of the religious education proposals will be to harden attitudes and to increase divisions and differences. This trend is actually already evident within the Jewish community where the demand for separate education has increased significantly over the last decade. Numbers of Jewish pupils in state schools are declining, due both to increased attendance at Jewish schools and the effects of a falling birthrate. This pattern is, however, more evident in the primary than in the secondary sector, and there are still many schools in areas of a high density of Jewish population where Jewish pupils form a high percentage. I personally think it unlikely that even in schools with a high percentage of Jewish pupils, parents and governors are going to be pressed for a modification of the nature of the assembly as described in the 1988 Education Reform Act.[1] It is far more likely that the old pattern of withdrawal will continue. It is significant that over the last ten years the whole area of organizing Jewish assemblies in state and private schools has become a much more important communal issue, the impetus for change actually coming from within the school population through such organizations as the Association for Jewish Sixth Formers.

A broader look at the changes caused by the Education Reform Act might reveal other areas of concern and potential conflict for the Jewish community. Already several Jewish voluntary aided schools have expressed their worries about the time demands a fully implemented national curriculum will make. Their concern is to maintain the level of religious education they currently provide, which is usually a minimum of 30 to 40 minutes a day and may reach a level of 40 per cent of the timetable in some schools. Moreover, several Jewish primary schools have begun teaching Jewish Studies in Modern Hebrew in recent years and there is, of course, no real suggestion as to the desirability of foreign language learning at primary level in the new legislation.

At secondary level, time could become an even more acute issue, particularly where parental desire for secular standards does not match the school's desire to transmit Jewish knowledge and commitment. This might seem an odd conflict to be describing in parents who have already made the choice of a Jewish school, but it highlights another possible area of conflict brought about by the Education Reform Act.

If, indeed, there is to be a return to some kind of 'grammar school' system (or at least image), as seems very likely in certain boroughs with high Jewish populations, then this could cause changes in the pattern of Jewish schooling. Many parents currently send their children to Jewish schools for negative rather than positive reasons – i.e. they *do not* want them to go to the local comprehensive. In areas where schools opt out and proclaim their return to some imagined golden age, many Jewish parents might again consider state schools as a natural option. This, in turn, will raise all the old questions of withdrawal from assemblies and from religious education. Why, it could be just like when I was at school.

References

1 *Education Reform Act, 1988,* Section 7, 6.

A Muslim response

Riadh El-Droubie

First of all I would like to say that I am pleased that the government of this country recognizes that a religious education is necessary to provide a firm base for society. Our belief is that morality and the social values of the society can only be based on a firm faith in God and a conviction of a religious order. We hope that the place given to Christianity will adhere to this and that the classroom will not be a place of indoctrination that other religions are 'untrue, inferior and that their believers are misguided people'.

The Muslim community did not spare an effort in responding to the Education Reform Bill of 1988 from the time it was first under study until today. Our aim is not to undermine the teaching of Christianity in schools. We accept the fact that it is the predominant faith of this country. However it should be recognized that Britain today is a multicultural and multi-faith society. It is our firm conviction that no believer should be expected to take part in an act of worship which indicates commitment to another faith, therefore each religious community should have the right to its own religious education.

The new Education Act has re-enacted some of the provisions of the 1944 Education Act namely, the right to withdraw children from instruction classes and from the assembly used for the act of worship. I am a firm believer that withdrawal of children from a class or an assembly will have a bad effect on the relationship between communities. Children will be subjected to segregation and intolerance, in addition to the confusion and the flexibility in interpretation of the articles of the Act. It may also add further fuel to the already existing racial discrimination. Let us hope that children, in particular the Christian children, will not become ignorant of their neighbours' tradition and religion. The support of the government to the minority communities to provide religious education in their own faith will enrich and contribute to the creation of tolerance, understanding and goodwill in our multicultural and multi-faith society.

The creation of an official Standing Advisory Council on Religious Education in the form stated will not solve the problem. There are quite a few schools where the majority, or a substantial number, of pupils are not Christian. Why should they suffer the lack of a proper education in their own faith until the SACRE approves or disapproves their request? They should be given the automatic right under the Act to hold their own religious classes and assembly. On this basis, the Muslim Education

Trust's official statement[1] of the basic educational concern of the Muslim community remains valid today. It called for:

1. The right to withdraw Muslim children from the collective worship and religious instruction.
2. Muslim children to be provided with the necessary facilities within the school premises to hold their Islamic assemblies and to receive Islamic education.
3. Section 26,(b) of the Education Act, 1944 to be amended to allow local education authorities to facilitate and meet the cost of religious worship and religious education of the minority faiths.
4. Suitable facilities to be provided by the local education authorities to Muslim children to offer their prayers in schools with ten or more Muslim pupils on its roll.
5. Muslim girls of secondary school age to be allowed to observe their religious rules to wear modest dress and headscarf conforming to the colour of the school uniform, in order to enable them to do their Islamic worship and attend Islamic religious education.[1]

It should be realized that it is not only religious education periods and the form of the assembly that we Muslims are worried about in this country. The moral values of subject lessons has been left out and the only emphasis considered is the materialist.

For this reason alone we believe that the only substitute left for the non-Christian communities who are worried about the education of their children is the denominational school. In such schools children could be brought up to believe in God, respect their parents, tolerate others and do their duty to the country where they live.

In conclusion, I would like to state that although I consider the withdrawal of children from any activity will widen the gap between communities, I find it very necessary in the present circumstance that Muslim children should be withdrawn from all religious classes or activities taking place at the school.

For us Muslims, there are many issues in the Education Reform Act of 1988 which need further clarification and discussion. Without any doubt the responsibility now rests with the Muslim community, i.e. parents, to take active part in their children's education. The mosque authority, as the official guardian, must advise and help parents to meet the challenge with knowledge and enlightenment and in an organized manner.

References

1 Muslim Education Trust (1988) *The Education Reform Act 1988: What Can Muslims Do?* London: Muslim Education Trust.

INDEX

Bedford Way Papers

ISSN 0261-0078